Best Easy Day Hikes Series

Best Easy Day Hikes
Rocky Mountain
National Park

Third Edition

Kent Da

publisher
FALCONGUIDES

GUILFORD, CONNECTICUT

FALCONGUIDES®

An imprint of The Rowman & Littlefield Publishing Group, Inc.
4501 Forbes Blvd., Ste. 200
Lanham, MD 20706
www.rowman.com
Falcon and FalconGuides are registered trademarks and Make Adventure Your Story is a trademark of The Rowman & Littlefield Publishing Group, Inc.

Distributed by NATIONAL BOOK NETWORK

Copyright © 2020 The Rowman & Littlefield Publishing Group, Inc.
Previous editions of this book were published by Falcon Publishing, Inc. in 2002 and 2014.

Maps by The Rowman & Littlefield Publishing Group, Inc.

British Library Cataloguing in Publication Information available

Library of Congress Cataloging-in-Publication Data available

ISBN 978-1-4930-4678-2 (paper : alk. paper)
ISBN 978-1-4930-4679-9 (electronic)

♾️™ The paper used in this publication meets the minimum requirements of American National Standard for Information Sciences—Permanence of Paper for Printed Library Materials, ANSI/NISO Z39.48-1992.

Contents

Introduction 1

   Maps 2

   Bear Lake Shuttle Bus Service 3

   Leave No Trace Ethics 4

   Trail Finder 8

Map Legend 10

Trails from Bear Lake Road

  1 Cub Lake 11

  2 The Pool 15

  3 Sprague Lake 19

  4 Alberta Falls 23

  5 The Loch 26

  6 Mills Lake 29

  7 Bear Lake Nature Trail 32

  8 Bierstadt Lake 35

  9 Lake Haiyaha 39

  10 Emerald Lake 43

Wild Basin Trails

  11 Ouzel Falls 47

  12 Allenspark Trail to Calypso Cascades 51

North End Trails

  13 Fall River Road 55

  14 Gem Lake 59

  15 Bridal Veil Falls 62

  16 West Creek Falls 66

Trails from Trail Ridge Road

  17 Timberline Pass 69

  18 Toll Memorial 72

  19 Fall River Pass to Milner Pass 76

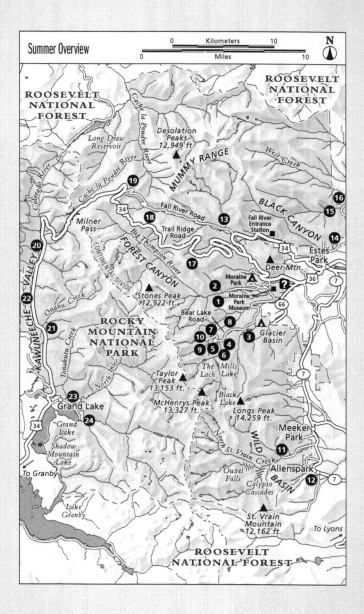

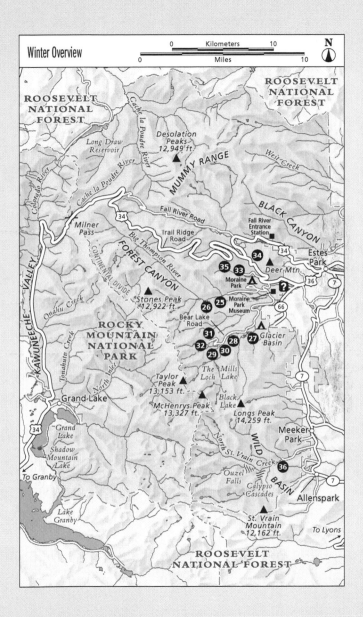

West Side Trails

20 Lulu City 80

21 Big Meadows 84

22 Coyote Valley 88

23 Cascade Falls 91

24 Adams Falls 95

Winter Trails

Introduction to Winter Trails 98

Moraine Park Trails

25 Winter Hike to Cub Lake 102

26 The Pool in Winter 106

Trails from Bear Lake Road

27 Skiing to Sprague Lake 110

28 Skiing from Glacier Gorge Trailhead to
    Sprague Lake 114

29 Loch Vale 118

30 Winter in Glacier Gorge 121

31 Bear Lake to Hallowell Park 124

32 Skiing to Emerald Lake 128

Trails from Trail Ridge Road

33 Upper Beaver Meadows in Winter 132

34 Winter Travel on Deer Mountain 136

35 Trail Ridge Road 140

Wild Basin Trail

36 Wild Basin in Winter 144

About the Author 147

Introduction

Hikers can approach Rocky Mountain National Park hiking trails in several different ways. I have written my previous guidebooks for visitors who return often to the park's trails and who seek to know the trail systems broadly and intimately. Rocky Mountain National Park may be unique among America's parklands in the number of visitors who return again and again, year after year. These repeat visitors raise their families on park trails and, in part, remember family histories in terms of their experiences while hiking Rocky Mountain National Park.

I once received a letter with two copies of a guidebook to autograph from a Chicago man. These were to be Christmas gifts for his grandsons (ages thirteen and sixteen), who had accomplished some rigorous hikes over the years. Evidently, these teens were asking for their own copies of my trail guide instead of relying on the various battered family editions. For him and thousands of other fans of Rocky Mountain National Park trails, I have written *Hiking Rocky Mountain National Park*.

However, many other hikers on Rocky Mountain National Park trails seek only to sample the richness of this park before moving on to other jewels in the scenic treasure spread lavishly across North America. No one has the time or opportunity to devote all the attention deserved by such wonders as Yellowstone, Grand Teton, North Cascades, Grand Canyon, Yosemite, and on and on. Whenever I visit Glacier National Park I am disappointed—because I have to leave.

Consider not only the national parks but also national monuments, wilderness areas, state parks, and other public lands. Several lifetimes would be too short to appreciate them in depth. The decision merely to sample the glories of Rocky Mountain National Park trails is difficult to dispute. For samplers I have written *Best Easy Day Hikes Rocky Mountain National Park.*

The changing seasons also cause different approaches to Rocky Mountain National Park trails. The vast bulk of trail use is in the normally ideal weather of summer and fall. Winter, though, also charms some Rocky Mountain National Park enthusiasts. Although snowshoes and cross-country skis never will equal the popularity of hiking boots, the joys of winter in the backcountry are as impossible to exaggerate as are the joys of summer. For those lucky enough to find themselves ready for the short days, hypnotic light, and long nights of the park's longest season, *Best Easy Day Hikes* is also a guide to sampling park trails in winter.

Maps

For both summer and winter backcountry travel, you may desire larger maps than those in this book. The most informative topographic map for the entire park is the National Geographic Trails Illustrated recreation map of Rocky Mountain National Park. It comes on water-resistant paper and shows 80 feet between contour lines.

For a 40-foot contour scale, turn to US Geological Survey quadrangle maps. These do not cover the entire park on one map. Each hike description includes the name of the quad (or quads) that cover that hike.

The Rocky Mountain Nature Association sells Trails Illustrated maps either from outlets at park visitor centers or by mail. The toll-free telephone number for the mail order department is (800) 816–0108. USGS quads are available online at https://store.usgs.gov.

Bear Lake Shuttle Bus Service

Rocky Mountain National Park offers free shuttle bus service to transport visitors through the popular Bear Lake and Moraine Park areas. Visitors can avoid the congested Bear Lake parking lot by parking at the Glacier Basin parking area or at the fairgrounds in Estes Park and catching the hikers' shuttle bus to Bear Lake. Hikers can use the bus as transportation between trailheads, facilitating one-way hikes, such as those beginning at Bear Lake and ending at Fern Lake Trailhead, Hollowell Park, Bierstadt Lake Trailhead, or Glacier Gorge Trailhead.

Bus service is daily in summer. The shuttle program goes to weekend-only service after Labor Day, serving visitors who want to view the aspens in their autumn colors during September. Schedules vary somewhat from year to year, but buses usually run every fifteen minutes from Glacier Basin in summer. The Moraine Park bus runs about once an hour.

The Bear Lake Shuttle makes intermediate stops at Bierstadt Lake Trailhead and Glacier Gorge Trailhead. The Moraine Park loop starts at the Fern Lake bus stop and runs to Glacier Basin parking lot with intermediate stops at Cub Lake Trailhead, Moraine Park Campground, Tuxedo Park, and Hollowell Park.

Since the shuttle began to run in 1978, proposals have been made to make its use compulsory for visiting Bear Lake during peak times. When compulsory use will be instituted is difficult to predict.

Leave No Trace Ethics

With increasing visitor use, both day and overnight, it is important to minimize our impacts and Leave No Trace of our visits into the backcountry. Please learn, practice, and pass on Leave No Trace skills and ethics to those you come in contact with. The following Leave No Trace principles will help protect precious backcountry resources.

Plan Ahead and Prepare

- Know and obey the regulations and special concerns for the area you'll visit.
- Be physically and mentally ready for your trip.
- Know the ability of every member of your group.
- Be informed of current weather conditions and other area information.
- Take responsibility for yourself and your group.
- Always leave an itinerary with someone at home.
- Choose proper equipment and clothing in subdued colors.
- Plan your meals and repackage food into reusable containers.

Travel and Camp on Durable Surfaces

While traveling . . .

- Stay on designated trails and hike single file. Never shortcut switchbacks.
- When traveling cross-country, choose the most durable surfaces available: rock, gravel, dry grasses, or snow. Spread out so that you don't grind a path where one didn't exist before.

- When you stop to rest, be careful not to mash vegetation. Sit on rocks, logs, or in clearings.

At camp . . .

- Be careful where you pitch your tent. Use the tent pad at the campsite, and camp in the camp area indicated on your permit.
- Restrict activities to areas where vegetation is compacted or absent.
- Use a large plastic water container to collect water so you don't need to make frequent trips to the water source.

Properly Dispose of Waste

- There are pit toilets at many backcountry sites. Use them.
- If there are no pit toilets nearby, urinate or defecate at least 200 feet (70 adult paces) from water, camp, or trails.
- Urinate in rocky places that won't be damaged by wildlife that dig for salts and minerals found in urine.
- Deposit human waste in catholes dug 6 to 8 inches deep. Carry a small garden trowel or lightweight scoop for digging. Cover and disguise the cathole when finished, or pack out solid waste.
- Use toilet paper sparingly and pack it out, along with sanitary napkins and tampons, in an airtight container.
- Wash your dishes and yourself at least 200 feet (70 adult paces) from water sources, and use small amounts, if any, of biodegradable soap. Scatter strained dishwater.
- Strain food scraps from wash water and pack them out.
- Pack everything you bring into the backcountry back out.

- Inspect your campsite for trash and evidence of your stay. Pack out all trash . . . yours and others'.

Leave What You Find

- Treat our natural heritage with respect. Leave plants, rocks, and historical artifacts as you find them.
- Good campsites are found, not made. Altering a site should not be necessary. Don't build structures or dig trenches.
- Let nature's sounds prevail. Speak softly and avoid making loud noises. Allow others to enjoy the peace and solitude of being in the backcountry.

Minimize Campfire Impacts

- Campfires are prohibited in the Rocky Mountain National Park wilderness except at certain designated campsites where metal fire rings are provided.
- Campfires can cause lasting impacts to the backcountry. Always use a lightweight, portable stove for cooking. A campfire is a luxury, not a necessity.
- Enjoy the sounds and wonders of the darkness, or use a candle lantern instead of a fire.
- Where fires are permitted, use the metal fire grate. Don't scar large rocks by using them to enlarge the fire area.
- Gather dead and down sticks, no larger than an adult's wrist, from a wide area, and leave them in their natural form until you are ready to burn them. Scatter any unused sticks.
- Do not snap branches off live, dead, or downed trees.
- Put out campfires completely.
- Remove and pack out all unburned trash from the fire

grate. Scatter the cold ashes over a large area well away from camp.

Respect Wildlife

- Enjoy wildlife at a distance.
- Never feed wildlife.
- Protect wildlife; hang your food and scented items securely.
- Minimize noise.
- Avoid sensitive habitat.

Be Considerate of Other Visitors

- Visit the backcountry in small parties. More people mean more impact.
- Avoid popular areas during times of high use.
- Avoid conflicts.
- Minimize noise.
- Keep a low profile.
- Take breaks and rest well off the trail, on a durable surface, of course.
- Yield to horse traffic.

For more information on Leave No Trace outdoor skills and ethics, visit the website at www.LNT.org. It's easy to enjoy and protect the backcountry simultaneously.

Trail Finder

Best Hikes for Great Views

    3   Sprague Lake
    5   The Loch
    7   Bear Lake Nature Trail
   10   Emerald Lake
   17   Timberline Pass
   18   Toll Memorial

Best Hikes for Waterfalls

    4   Alberta Falls
   11   Ouzel Falls
   12   Allenspark Trail to Calypso Cascades
   15   Bridal Veil Falls
   16   West Creek Falls
   23   Cascade Falls
   24   Adams Falls

Best Hikes with Children

    3   Sprague Lake
    4   Alberta Falls
    7   Bear Lake Nature Trail
   10   Emerald Lake
   11   Ouzel Falls
   14   Gem Lake
   18   Toll Memorial
   24   Adams Falls

Best Hikes for Wildlife

1   Cub Lake
15   Bridal Veil Falls
33   Upper Beaver Meadows in Winter

Best Hikes for Photographers

3   Sprague Lake
5   The Loch
6   Mills Lake
10   Emerald Lake
11   Ouzel Falls
14   Gem Lake
17   Timberline Pass

Best Summit Hikes

18   Toll Memorial
34   Winter Travel on Deer Mountain

Best Hikes for Solitude

15   Bridal Veil Falls
16   West Creek Falls

Map Legend

—⟨34⟩—	US Highway
—⟨278⟩—	State Highway
————	Local Road
= = = = =	Unimproved Road
▬▬▬▬▬	Featured Trail
- - - - - -	Trail
— ·· — ·· —	Continental Divide
— · — · — ·	National Forest/Park Boundary
～～～	River/Creek
⬭	Body of Water
▲	Campground
⁞	Gate
▲	Mountain/Peak
♠	Park
🄿	Parking
⤳	Pass
🄵	Picnic Area
■	Point of Interest/Structure
🄸	Ranger Station
🚻	Restrooms
❶	Trailhead
○	Town/City
🖼	Viewpoint/Overlook
❓	Visitor/Information Center
⋙	Waterfall

1 Cub Lake

The Cub Lake Trail meanders across a meadow recovering well from wildfire damage, then it climbs through burned forest to the lake, still displaying yellow pond lilies.

Start: Cub Lake Trailhead
Distance: 6.3-mile loop
Hiking time: 5 hours
Difficulty: Easy
Trail surface: Dirt
Best season: Summer
Other trail users: Equestrians
Canine compatibility: Dogs are prohibited
Fees and permits: No fees besides park entrance fee
Trail contact: Rocky Mountain National Park Backcountry Office, 1000 US Hwy 36, Estes Park; (970) 586-1242; www.nps.gov/romo
Maps: Trails Illustrated Rocky Mountain National Park; USGS McHenrys Peak and Longs Peak
Highlights: Wildflowers, wildlife, Cub Lake
Wildlife: Many bird species, mule deer, marmot, golden-mantled ground squirrel, many butterfly species
Cub Lake Trailhead elevation: 8,080 feet
Cub Lake elevation: 8,630 feet

Finding the trailhead: From the Beaver Meadows entrance (US 36), drive 0.2 mile to Bear Lake Road. Turn left and follow Bear Lake Road for 1.2 miles, then turn right toward Moraine Park Campground. Follow the signs for 2.2 miles to the Cub Lake Trailhead and three reasonably convenient parking areas. GPS: N40 21.40' / W105 36.90'

The Hike

From the trailhead, hike south on the Cub Lake Trail, among the richest in the park for the wildflowers and wildlife seen

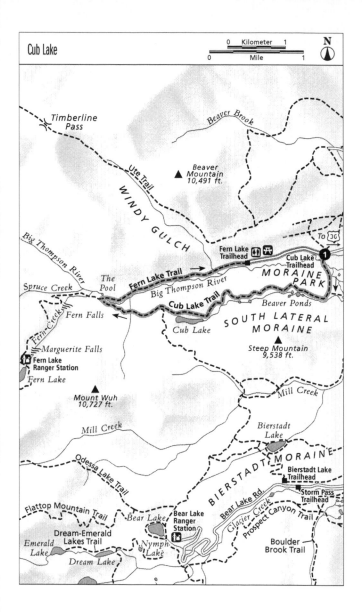

along its length. For much of its route across the level floor of Moraine Park, the trail is extremely easy to walk. Spoiled by the initial easiness of the trail, hikers may think the last 0.5 mile is rather steep.

Jammed with innumerable opportunities for close-up photos, the Cub Lake Trail is not notable for its scenery, compared with much of the rest of the park. Low scenery potential and extensive opportunities for studying the small, intimate details that are abundant along the way to Cub Lake make this an ideal trail for cloudy-day hiking. Insect repellent may be beneficial.

A December 2012 wildfire actually improved much wildflower habitat by opening former forest to sunlight. The wetlands through which the trail initially passes is recovering as new growth rises from the roots of burned water birch. Rare wood lilies, their bulbs hidden beneath the ground, also emerged again to display their spotted orange grandeur.

The best view is looking toward Stones Peak from the east end of the lake, which is reached after 2.3 miles. Although the 2012 forest fire did nothing to help the vista, the vegetation growing back exemplifies plant succession after a fire or other disturbance. The water lilies on the lake's surface denote the gradual filling in of Cub Lake. Baby mallards among the lily pads are delightful; the lake's leeches (which don't prey on humans) are less lovely.

Another 1.4 miles beyond Cub Lake, the trail meets the Fern Lake Trail, forming a circle route of 6.3 miles, including nearly a mile of road walking between the Cub and Fern Lake Trailheads.

Miles and Directions

0.0 Start at Cub Lake Trailhead.

0.5 At trail junction where trail used mainly by horses goes left, turn right onto trail to Cub Lake.

2.2 From the east end of Cub Lake is a view of Stones Peak rising above the far end of the lake.

2.7 Trail to Mill Creek Basin cuts left. Continue right to Fern Lake Trail.

3.7 At Fern Lake Trail, a left turn leads to Fern Falls; a right soon reaches The Pool in the Big Thompson River at a bridge.

5.4 Reach Fern Lake Trailhead; cross small dirt parking lot to aspen-shaded road back to Cub Lake Trailhead.

6.3 Arrive back at Cub Lake Trailhead.

2 The Pool

The first 2 miles of the Fern Lake Trail follow whitewater on an easy grade along the Big Thompson River to a quiet spot below a timber bridge buttressed by granite outcrops.

Start: Fern Lake Trailhead
Hiking time: 3 hours
Distance: 3.4 miles out-and-back
Difficulty: Easy
Trail surface: Dirt
Best season: Summer
Other trail users: Equestrians
Canine compatibility: Dogs are prohibited
Fees and permits: No fees besides park entrance fee
Trail contacts: Rocky Mountain National Park Backcountry Office, 1000 US Hwy 36, Estes Park;
(970) 586-1242; www.nps.gov/romo
Maps: Trails Illustrated Rocky Mountain National Park; USGS McHenrys Peak
Highlights: Arch Rocks, The Pool
Wildlife: Mule deer, chipmunk, red squirrel, water ouzel
Fern Lake Trailhead elevation: 8,155 feet
The Pool elevation: 8,320 feet

Finding the trailhead: From the Beaver Meadows entrance of Rocky Mountain National Park on US 36, drive 0.2 mile to Bear Lake Road. Turn left and follow Bear Lake Road for 1.2 miles, then turn right toward Moraine Park Campground. Drive another 0.5 mile and turn left just before reaching the campground. The pavement ends after 1.2 miles; continue another 2 miles to the end of the unpaved road. GPS: N40 21.294' / W105 37.854'

The Hike

Fern Lake, Fern Creek, and Fern Falls were probably named after a local lady rather than after the many bracken ferns that grow along the trail to The Pool, which follows a very easy grade along the Big Thompson River. These ferns grow in stream valleys, where moisture is readily available. Look closely at the lacy patterns of the fern leaves, which are particularly lovely in fall when they turn a rusty golden color.

The Fern Lake Trail often emerges from the forest into meadows opened by beavers removing aspen. Throughout the warm months, these meadows produce many wildflowers that brighten the open spots with masses of color.

Many huge rocks border the trail, some carried to their resting places within the ice of glaciers flowing from the Continental Divide, occasionally visible ahead. Even more boulders, those not rounded by grinding ice, fell to their present spots after the ice melted. Rocky debris fans down the slopes, some of the older rockfalls mellowed by invading trees and shrubs. A rockfall from July 2013 is easy to see where the trail passes between towering megaliths called Arch Rocks.

Visible from the trail is the slope across the river burned by a 2012 forest fire. In one spot, as the trail approaches The Pool, the fire jumped the river and burned trees through which the trail passes. Many other dead trees line the trail, not killed by fire but by mountain pine beetles, stockpiling fuel for future conflagrations.

The Pool is a wide spot where a bridge crosses the Big Thompson River, providing a sturdy platform for viewing swirling patterns of white water. Rock ledges at water's edge here often are nest sites for water ouzels, entertaining gray birds that live entirely within spray distance of water. An ouzel enters its moss-domed nest through a hole in the nest's side. You may find an inconspicuous nest by watching a bird repeatedly fly back and forth to the same spot along the stream.

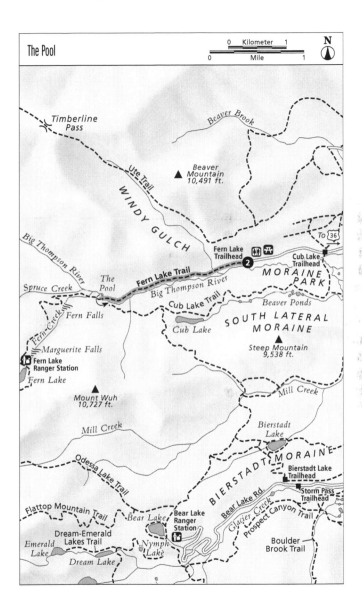

The Pool

0   Kilometer   1

0   Mile   1

N

Timberline Pass

Beaver Brook

Ute Trail

Beaver Mountain
10,491 ft.

WINDY GULCH

Big Thompson River

Fern Lake Trailhead

Cub Lake Trailhead

To 36

MORAINE PARK

The Pool

Spruce Creek

Fern Lake Trail

Big Thompson River

Cub Lake Trail

Beaver Ponds

Fern Creek

Fern Falls

Cub Lake

SOUTH LATERAL MORAINE

Marguerite Falls

Fern Lake Ranger Station

Fern Lake

Steep Mountain
9,538 ft.

Mount Wuh
10,727 ft.

Mill Creek

Mill Creek

Bierstadt Lake

Odessa Lake Trail

BIERSTADT MORAINE

Bierstadt Lake Trailhead

Storm Pass Trailhead

Flattop Mountain Trail

Bear Lake

Bear Lake Ranger Station

Bear Lake Rd.

Glacier Creek

Prospect Canyon Trail

Dream-Emerald Lakes Trail

Nymph Lake

Boulder Brook Trail

Emerald Lake

Dream Lake

Miles and Directions

0.0 Start at Fern Lake Trailhead.

1.5 Pass between Arch Rocks, which are megaliths beside the trail rather than an arch over the trail.

1.7 Arrive at the substantial rock and timber bridge over the Big Thompson River at The Pool.

3.4 Arrive back at Fern Lake Trailhead.

3 Sprague Lake

The loop trail around Sprague Lake is nearly flat and very easy to walk. It provides many photography opportunities of the Front Range, especially in the early morning.

Start: Sprague Lake Picnic Area
Hiking time: 1 hour
Distance: 0.7-mile loop
Difficulty: Easy
Trail surface: Packed earth
Best season: Summer
Other trail users: Wheelchairs
Canine compatibility: Dogs are prohibited
Fees and permits: No fees besides park entrance fee
Trail contacts: Rocky Mountain National Park Backcountry Office,
1000 US Hwy 36, Estes Park; (970) 586-1242; www.nps.gov/romo
Maps: Trails Illustrated Rocky Mountain National Park; USGS Longs Peak
Highlights: Views of Front Range, beaver ponds
Wildlife: Red squirrel, mallard duck, golden-mantled ground squirrel, gray jay, Steller's jay
Sprague Lake elevation: 8,710 feet

Finding the trailhead: The Sprague Lake Picnic Area is about 6.5 miles along Bear Lake Road from US 36. A sign indicates a turn to the left from Bear Lake Road. GPS: N40 9.219' / W105 36.525'

The Hike

Gray jays, Steller's jays, and sometimes Clark's nutcrackers hang around the picnic area at the Sprague Lake parking lot, waiting to steal unguarded morsels. Try to photograph these birds in the low branches that serve as their lookout points, which gives a much nicer background than a picnic bench or the scantily vegetated ground.

Mallard ducks here are very tame and easy to photograph. Try for some action instead of the typical static pose: stretching a wing, interacting with other ducks, swimming among attractive shoreline grasses. In the spring you can often photograph cute baby mallards at Sprague Lake. Try using them also as silhouettes in the foreground of pictures of the Front Range from the east side of the lake.

Walking around the lake provides at least two good perspectives of Otis Peak, Hallett Peak, and Flattop Mountain in the Front Range. The chances for reflections of the mountains on a still lake surface are excellent early in the day. The first good spot, if you begin walking left on the north side, is in a sheltered cove where a stream exits the 13-acre lake. Pines form a dark-shadowed frame for the mountains, the silhouetted needles filling empty sky with interesting shapes and directing the eye to the mountains.

Also here is one of the most photogenic blue spruces in the area. This single example of Colorado's state tree presents a classic cone shape when viewed from the east, across the water, and stands out nicely from the surrounding lodgepole pines.

The second good viewpoint of the Front Range is at the east end of the lake at its second outlet. There are few trees here to serve as good foreground for pictures of the mountains, but you can use bushes or flowers along the shore for this purpose. Rounded boulders that were deposited by a melting glacier sit in the water near the shore. The round shapes of these granite rocks make an interesting foreground element to add depth to your photo.

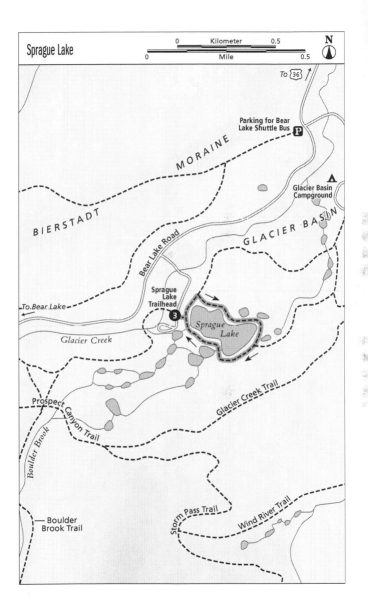

Sprague Lake

N

| 0 | Kilometer | 0.5 |

| 0 | Mile | 0.5 |

To 36

Parking for Bear
Lake Shuttle Bus P

MORAINE

Glacier Basin
Campground

BIERSTADT

GLACIER BASIN

Bear Lake Road

Sprague
Lake
Trailhead

To Bear Lake

3

Sprague
Lake

Glacier Creek

Prospect Canyon Trail

Glacier Creek Trail

Boulder Brook

Boulder
Brook Trail

Storm Pass Trail

Wind River Trail

Miles and Directions

0.0 Start a short way east of Sprague Lake Picnic Area. Go left, as described, for best photo spots; right for easiest surface to wheelchair accessible camp site.

0.3 Trail branches left to follow outlet stream; continue right along lakeshore.

0.4 Trail branches left a short way to wheelchair-accessible backcountry campsite; continue right along lakeshore.

0.7 Arrive back at Sprague Lake Picnic Area.

4 Alberta Falls

The hike to Alberta Falls follows a well–constructed path to one of the park's most photographed waterfalls.

Start: Glacier Gorge Trailhead
Hiking time: 2 hours
Distance: 1.8 miles out-and-back
Difficulty: Easy
Trail surface: Dirt
Best season: Summer
Other trail users: Equestrians
Canine compatibility: Dogs are prohibited
Fees and permits: No fees besides park entrance fee
Trail contacts: Rocky Mountain National Park Backcountry Office, 1000 US Hwy 36, Estes Park; (970) 586-1242; www.nps.gov/romo
Maps: Trails Illustrated Rocky Mountain National Park; USGS McHenrys Peak
Highlights: Alberta Falls
Wildlife: Mule deer, red squirrel, golden-mantled ground squirrel, chipmunk
Glacier Gorge Trailhead elevation: 9,240 feet
Alberta Falls elevation: 9,400 feet

Finding the trailhead: Glacier Gorge Trailhead is 8 miles up Bear Lake Road from US 36. If the parking lot is full, drive another mile to a larger parking area and hike to Glacier Gorge Trailhead via a 0.4-mile path (the horse trail) marked at the east end of the parking area or via a marked branch from the Dream Lake Trail just south of Bear Lake. Along the trail connecting Bear Lake and Glacier Gorge parking areas, late June hikers may encounter very rare brownie lady's-slipper orchids. GPS: N40 18.671' / W105 38.362'

The Hike

This easy path to a waterfall is one of the most popular short hikes in Rocky Mountain National Park. Along the way to Alberta Falls are many aspen that grew after a 1900 forest

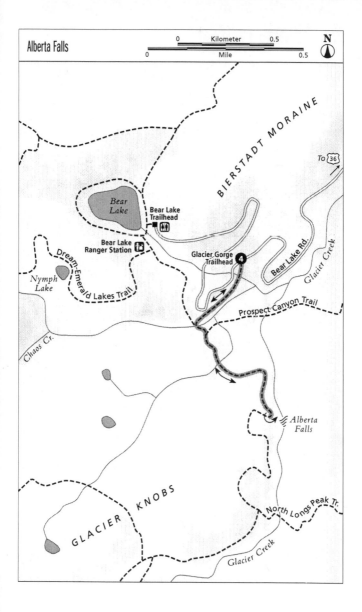

Alberta Falls

0   Kilometer   0.5

0   Mile   0.5

N

B I E R S T A D T   M O R A I N E

To 36

Bear
Lake

Bear Lake
Trailhead

Bear Lake
Ranger Station

Glacier Gorge
Trailhead 4

Bear Lake Rd.

Glacier Creek

Dream-Emerald Lakes Trail

Nymph
Lake

Chaos Cr.

Prospect Canyon Trail

Alberta
Falls

G L A C I E R   K N O B S

North Longs Peak Tr.

Glacier Creek

fire. Particularly with their fall color, these trees make this an extremely pleasant trail.

Heavy use has dictated that a certain percentage of the throngs, those who are ignorant of proper wilderness behavior, have carved their initials on the white aspen bark along this trail. Thankfully, most of this damage appears to be fairly old. The hiking public today seems to be more sophisticated about wilderness ethics, but even a tiny percentage of vandals can mess things up quite a bit.

Autumn aspens look their best when viewed from the southeast or southwest so your eyes catch the sunlight coming through the translucent leaves, creating a stained-glass-window effect. When leaves are backlit, golden color shimmers with greater intensity. With your back to the sun, you will notice duller autumn colors in all deciduous trees and bushes.

Abner Sprague, a pioneer and one of the first lodge owners in this area, named Alberta Falls for his wife. The falls plunge over a ledge gouged by glaciers. Other signs of glacial passing are boulders, gravel, light-colored clay, and bare bedrock smoothed by the moving ice. Also near the falls are now-dry potholes in the rock shaped by grinding stones carried by meltwater from retreating glaciers. This roaring torrent of ancestral Glacier Creek was much more formidable than today's stream, which still throws cooling spray on nearby hikers.

Miles and Directions

0.0 Head down path from Glacier Gorge Trailhead.

0.9 Arrive Alberta Falls.

1.8 Arrive back at Glacier Gorge Trailhead.

5 The Loch

By virtue of its euphonious name, Loch Vale Trail draws many hikers beyond Alberta Falls. None are disappointed by the magnificent views of cliff-bound peaks above a glacier-carved lake—The Loch.

Start: Glacier Gorge Trailhead

Hiking time: About 5 hours

Distance: 6.0 miles out-and-back

Difficulty: Moderately easy

Trail surface: Dirt

Best season: Summer

Other trail users: Equestrians as far as 3-way trail junction 2.2 miles from trailhead

Canine compatibility: Dogs are prohibited

Fees and permits: No fees besides park entrance fee

Trail contacts: Rocky Mountain National Park Backcountry Office, 1000 US Hwy 36, Estes Park; (970) 586-1242; www.nps.gov/romo

Maps: Trails Illustrated Rocky Mountain National Park; USGS McHenrys Peak

Highlights: Alberta Falls, The Loch

Wildlife: Mule deer, golden-mantled ground squirrel, pika, yellow-bellied marmot, gray jay, Clark's nutcracker, water ouzel

Glacier Gorge Trailhead elevation: 9,240 feet

The Loch elevation: 10,180 feet

Finding the trailhead: Glacier Gorge Trailhead is 8 miles up Bear Lake Road from US 36. If lot is full, drive another 0.7 mile to a larger parking area and hike to Glacier Gorge Trailhead via a 0.4-mile path (the horse trail) marked at the east end of parking area or via a marked branch from the Dream Lake Trail just south of Bear Lake. GPS: N40 8.671' / W105 38.362'

The Hike

Estes Park pioneer Abner Sprague used a pun to name The Loch and Loch Vale, the valley in which this photogenic

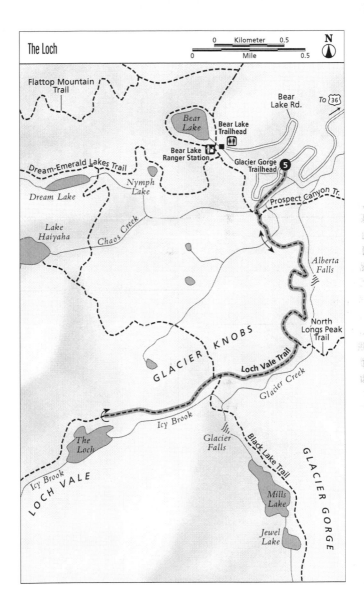

The Loch

Kilometer 0 0.5
Mile 0 0.5

N

Flattop Mountain Trail

Bear Lake

Bear Lake Trailhead

Bear Lake Ranger Station

Dream-Emerald Lakes Trail

Nymph Lake

Dream Lake

Glacier Gorge Trailhead

Bear Lake Rd.

To 36

5

Prospect Canyon Tr.

Lake Haiyaha

Chaos Creek

Alberta Falls

North Longs Peak Trail

GLACIER KNOBS

Loch Vale Trail

Glacier Creek

The Loch

Icy Brook

Glacier Falls

Black Lake Trail

GLACIER GORGE

U.S. 36

Icy Brook

LOCH VALE

Mills Lake

Jewel Lake

lake sits. He named these features for a guest at his lodge, a banker named Locke. Sprague changed the spelling to *loch,* the Scottish word for lake, a clever joke that causes some confusion a century later. But many people who judge this to be the prettiest lake in Rocky Mountain National Park think calling it The Lake is appropriate.

Named for Sprague's wife, Alberta Falls may be the most-photographed falls in the park. Beyond the falls the trail climbs amid rocks through land slowly recovering from a 1900 forest fire. Watch for colorful wildflowers growing against burned, weathered wood.

In the rock fields where the trail levels then descends slightly, marmots and pikas may whistle and chirp at passing hikers but likely will not permit close approach.

In a forested bowl missed by the 1900 fire, the trail splits three ways. A sign indicates the middle way goes to The Loch. A 0.5 mile beyond the junction, Icy Brook tumbles with a view of Taylor Peak above.

Taylor Glacier, nearby snowfields, and the Cathedral Wall dominate views from The Loch. Twisted limber pines on the rocky shore create a dramatic foreground.

Miles and Directions

- **0.0** Head down the trail from Glacier Gorge Trailhead.
- **0.9** Arrive at Alberta Falls.
- **2.2** Trail splits; take middle trail to The Loch in Loch Vale. (Left trail goes to Glacier Gorge; right to Lake Haiyaha.)
- **3.0** Arrive at The Loch.
- **6.0** Arrive back at Glacier Gorge Trailhead.

6 Mills Lake

This very popular hike leads to a rock-rimmed lake situated dramatically below Longs Peak and the extremely jagged Keyboard of the Winds.

Start: Glacier Gorge Trailhead
Hiking time: 4 hours
Distance: 5.6 miles out-and-back
Difficulty: Moderately easy
Trail surface: Dirt
Best season: Summer
Other trail users: Equestrians as far as a three-way trail junction 2.2 miles from the trailhead
Canine compatibility: Dogs are prohibited
Fees and permits: No fees besides park entrance fee
Trail contacts: Rocky Mountain National Park Backcountry Office, 1000 US Hwy 36, Estes Park;
(970) 586-1242; www.nps.gov/romo
Maps: Trails Illustrated Rocky Mountain National Park; USGS McHenrys Peak
Highlights: Alberta Falls, Mills Lake
Wildlife: Mule deer, golden-mantled ground squirrel, gray jay, Clark's nutcracker, pika, yellow-bellied marmot, water ouzel
Glacier Gorge Trailhead elevation: 9,240 feet
Mills Lake elevation: 9,940 feet

Finding the trailhead: Glacier Gorge Trailhead is 8 miles up the Bear Lake Road from US 36. GPS: N40 18.671' / W105 38.362'

The Hike

Mills Lake is named for Enos Mills, the father of Rocky Mountain National Park. Mills wrote many articles and books (most still in print) and gave many lectures urging the establishment of a national park around Longs Peak. Six years of concentrated effort resulted in the park's creation in 1915.

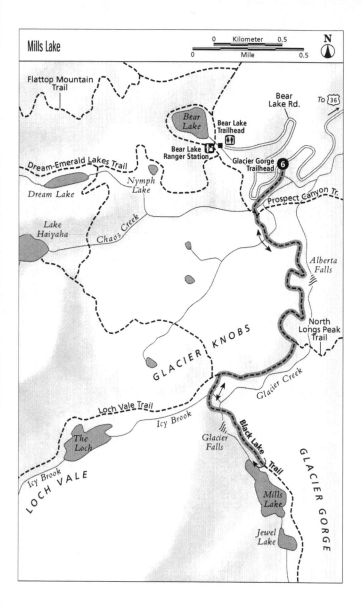

Many hikers consider Mills Lake the prettiest lake in the park, a bold claim where there are so many outstanding contenders for this praise. Without doubt, this popular destination is extremely lovely in its dramatic setting below Longs Peak.

Along the first mile of the trail, Glacier Creek is exciting, especially where it shoots over Alberta Falls. Also along the first part of the trail, notice the weather-etched patterns in the grain of red, gray, and black wood killed in a 1900 forest fire.

Scrambling over glacier-scoured bedrock in Glacier Gorge, you will see several spectacular views of Longs Peak, tallest in the park, and the jagged Keyboard of the Winds. The round boulders left isolated on the bedrock by melting glaciers and the twisted shapes of limber pines increase the interest of this scene.

Unlike most lakes on the east side of the national park, Mills Lake is prettiest in the late afternoon. This fact alone is enough to merit praise from hikers who are tired of rising before dawn to see the best light on the peaks. Afternoon skies frequently contain clouds, which can either add interesting shapes to an empty sky or throw the entire landscape into muted shadow.

Miles and Directions

0.0 Head down the trail from Glacier Gorge Trailhead.

0.9 Arrive at Alberta Falls.

2.2 Trail splits; turn left to Mills Lake in Glacier Gorge. (The middle trail goes to Loch Vale; the right to Lake Haiyaha.)

2.8 Arrive at Mills Lake.

5.6 Arrive back at Glacier Gorge Trailhead.

7 Bear Lake Nature Trail

This path perambulates the perimeter of the park's most popular lake.

Start: Bear Lake parking area
Hiking time: 1 hour
Distance: 0.5-mile loop
Difficulty: Easy
Trail surface: Dirt
Best seasons: Summer and fall
Other trail users: Human foot traffic only
Canine compatibility: Dogs are prohibited
Fees and permits: No fees besides park entrance fee
Trail contacts: Rocky Mountain National Park Backcountry Office, 1000 US Hwy 36, Estes Park;
(970) 586-1242; www.nps.gov/romo
Maps: Trails Illustrated Rocky Mountain National Park; USGS McHenrys Peak
Highlights: Views of Hallett Peak and Longs Peak, natural history points of interest
Wildlife: Mountain chickadee, red squirrel, golden-mantled ground squirrel, chipmunk, Steller's jay, gray jay, Clark's nutcracker
Bear Lake elevation: 9,475 feet

Finding the trailhead: Bear Lake is 9 miles from the Beaver Meadows entrance (US 36) to Rocky Mountain National Park at the end of Bear Lake Road. GPS: N40 18.698' / W105 38.674'

The Hike

The mostly level trail around Bear Lake is very popular. Nonetheless, it offers many opportunities for unspoiled views as well as photographs of the landscape, close-ups of patterns on tree trunks and boulders, wildlife portraits, and dramatic settings for people pictures.

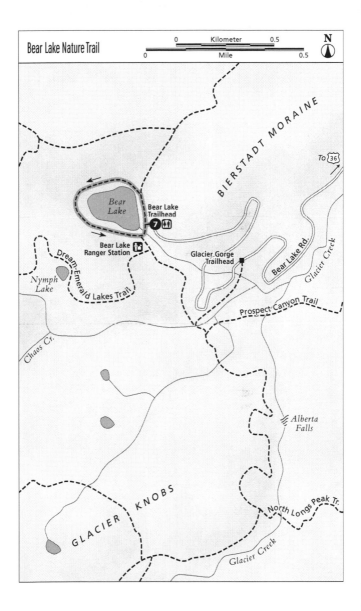

Bear Lake Nature Trail

N

0   Kilometer   0.5
0   Mile   0.5

BIERSTADT MORAINE

To 36

Bear Lake

Bear Lake Trailhead
7

Bear Lake Ranger Station

Glacier Gorge Trailhead

Bear Lake Rd.

Glacier Creek

Dream-Emerald Lakes Trail

Nymph Lake

Prospect Canyon Trail

Chaos Cr.

Alberta Falls

GLACIER KNOBS

North Longs Peak Tr.

Glacier Creek

Thirty-two numbered posts around the lake indicate points of interest, with short but informative descriptions in a booklet available from a dispenser at the east end of the lake. This reference is handy for anyone walking around Bear Lake. The more you know about what you see, the more likely you are to enjoy it and to notice things you otherwise might have overlooked.

Early morning is the best time to view the east end of the lake, where most people congregate. Arriving early will help you avoid crowds and also enable you to view shadowed trees and boulders in the foreground as interesting silhouettes framing rugged cliffs above.

Heading counterclockwise around the lake will give you the most opportunities for interesting views of Hallett Peak. Fences protect some areas from trampling feet; walkers should stay on the trail. Also along the east side of the lake, look for interesting grain patterns in weathered limber pines. Be sure to notice the patterns of gneiss, a type of rock pointed out at stop ten.

Around stop twelve are magnificent views across the lake to Longs Peak and the other high mountains surrounding Glacier Gorge. This perspective of Longs is best enjoyed in late afternoon. Any time of day, however, is a wonderful time to enjoy the beauty the Bear Lake area has to offer.

Miles and Directions

0.0 Walk west from Bear Lake parking lot about 200 yards up to Bear Lake. Follow trail with its numbered stakes to the right (counterclockwise) around the lakeshore.

0.5 Complete loop around Bear Lake.

8 Bierstadt Lake

After a short climb, this walkway wanders through the woods to a uniquely formed lake.

Start: Bear Lake Trailhead
Hiking time: 4 hours
Difficulty: Moderately easy
Distance: 3.0-mile shuttle
Trail surface: Dirt
Best season: Fall
Other trail users: Equestrians, except on Bear Lake Nature Trail
Canine compatibility: Dogs are prohibited
Fees and permits: No fees besides park entrance fee
Trail contacts: Rocky Mountain National Park Backcountry Office; 1000 US Hwy 36, Estes Park; (970) 586-1242; www.nps.gov/romo

Maps: Trails Illustrated Rocky Mountain National Park; USGS McHenrys Peak and Longs Peak
Highlights: Views of Hallett and Longs Peaks from Bear Lake, views of Longs Peak from Bierstadt Lake, aspen along south side of Bierstadt Moraine
Wildlife: Mule deer, elk, gray jay
Bear Lake Trailhead elevation: 9,475 feet
Bierstadt Lake Trailhead elevation: 8,850 feet
High point between Bear and Bierstadt Lakes: 9,730 feet

Finding the trailhead: Begin at Bear Lake, the end of Bear Lake Road 9.0 miles from US 36. GPS: N40 18.67' / W105 38.67'

Park the shuttle car at Bierstadt Lake Trailhead, 6.4 miles along Bear Lake Road from US 36. GPS: N40 20.49' / W105 36.31'

The Hike

Bierstadt Lake's formation may be unique among the lakes of Rocky Mountain National Park: It rests in a basin formed by the merging of two lateral moraines, rock ridges dumped by glaciers as they flowed down mountain valleys.

Most of the park's lakes were made by glaciers, but in ways that set them beneath scenic peaks. Bierstadt just sits in the midst of woods, although the view across from the north shore toward Longs Peak in the distance is not bad. It seems ironic that comparatively mundane Bierstadt Lake was named for a nineteenth-century painter whose Rocky Mountain scenes were very grandiose.

The hike to the lake demonstrates how the journey can be more important than the destination. The best way is to begin at Bear Lake and follow a trail with only 255 feet elevation gain up Bierstadt Moraine. The nature trail around Bear Lake offers excellent views of Hallett Peak in the morning and an even better picture of Longs Peak in the afternoon. For the view of Longs, you need to walk past the Flattop Mountain Trail, which begins the trail to Bierstadt Lake, and continue for a few more yards around Bear Lake. Branching from the Flattop Mountain Trail 0.4 mile from Bear Lake, the Bierstadt Lake Trail continues climbing a short way through aspen to its high point. Then you descend through lovely woods to a gentle grade atop Bierstadt Moraine.

The area around Bierstadt Lake is a maze of trails, but signs provide adequate guidance. One trail circles the lake, another descends to Hollowell Park, a third heads down to the Bear Lake Shuttle parking area. But the best route of descent is to the Bierstadt Lake Trailhead on Bear Lake Road, 1.4 miles from the lake. Hikers reach the point of descent by following the trail around the lake's west end to a marked junction on the south side of the lake. From this junction, the Bierstadt Lake Trail switchbacks through open

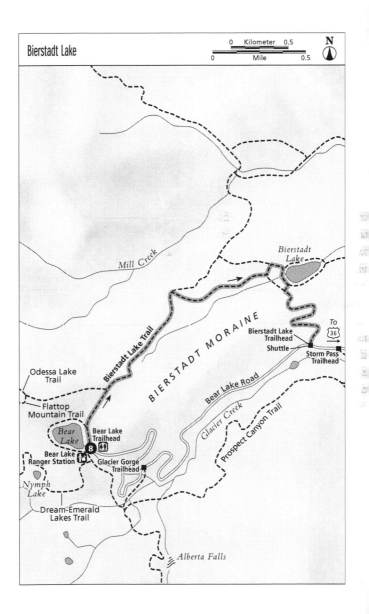

Bierstadt Lake

Mill Creek

Bierstadt Lake

Bierstadt Lake Trail

BIERSTADT MORAINE

To 36

Bierstadt Lake Trailhead

Shuttle

Storm Pass Trailhead

Odessa Lake Trail

Flattop Mountain Trail

Bear Lake Road

Glacier Creek

Prospect Canyon Trail

Bear Lake

Bear Lake Trailhead

8

Bear Lake Ranger Station

Glacier Gorge Trailhead

Nymph Lake

Dream-Emerald Lakes Trail

Alberta Falls

0   Kilometer   0.5
0   Mile   0.5

N

lodgepole pine and aspen woods that grew up after a 1900 forest fire. Nice at any time of year, this trail is magic in autumn when aspen leaves have turned golden.

Descending the trail causes hikers to face mostly south, increasing the richness of color in the aspen leaves as the sun shines through them. Mountains in the distance form interesting silhouettes, dark and brooding backgrounds that make the leaves stand out all the more brilliantly. The more dramatic peaks are to the southwest, making afternoon the most spectacular time on the south face of Bierstadt Moraine. Catch the shuttle back to Bear Lake or arrange for other transportation during the months when the shuttle does not run.

Miles and Directions

0.0 Start at Bear Lake and go right on Bear Lake Nature Trail.

0.1 Turn right at trail up Flattop Mountain Trail junction.

0.4 Trail divides; take right branch toward Bierstadt Lake. (The left branch heads to Flattop Mountain.)

1.0 Trail splits; take right branch toward Bierstadt Lake. (Left branch leads down to Mill Creek Basin.)

1.3 Trail splits again (be thankful for trail marking signs); go left toward the north side of Bierstadt Lake to another trail split. Turn right toward the lake for a photo of Longs Peak (left goes down to Mill Creek Basin), then circle to the south side of Bierstadt Lake for the descent to Bierstadt Lake Trailhead.

1.6 Arrive at southwest end of Bierstadt Lake. (Trail circles lakeshore; branch at east end descends to shuttle parking lot across Bear Lake Road from Glacier Basin Campground.)

3.0 Arrive at Bierstadt Lake Trailhead.

9 Lake Haiyaha

Often crowded on the first half, much less so on the second, this trail climbs and descends to a lovely lake whose name is challenging to pronounce and worse to spell.

Start: Bear Lake parking area
Hiking time: 4 hours
Distance: 4.2 miles out-and-back
Difficulty: Moderately easy
Trail surface: Asphalt to dirt
Best season: Summer
Other trail users: Human foot traffic only
Canine compatibility: Dogs are prohibited
Fees and permits: No fees besides park entrance fee
Trail contacts: Rocky Mountain National Park Backcountry Office, 1000 US Hwy 36, Estes Park; (970) 586-1242; www.nps.gov/romo

Maps: Trails Illustrated Rocky Mountain National Park; USGS McHenrys Peak
Highlights: Nymph Lake, Dream Lake, Longs Peak/Glacier Gorge views, Lake Haiyaha
Wildlife: Mule deer, golden-mantled ground squirrel, chipmunks, yellow-bellied marmot, Clark's nutcracker
Bear Lake Trailhead elevation: 9,475 feet
Lake Haiyaha elevation: 10,220 feet
High point of hike: 10,240 feet

Finding the trailhead: From the Beaver Meadows entrance to the park, take US 36 to Bear Lake Road and drive 9 miles to the road's end at the Bear Lake Trailhead. GPS: N40 18.698' / W105 38.674'

The Hike

The first half of the hike to Lake Haiyaha follows one of the most popular (and crowded) trails in Rocky Mountain

National Park. Avoid the crowds and experience the trail at its best by starting early in the day, as soon after sunrise as you can bear.

At the beginning of the hike, there are striking views of Hallett Peak above Bear Lake, seen by detouring a few yards from the Dream Lake Trail. The best views at Bear Lake probably are a short distance to the right from where you reach the shore.

The hike to Haiyaha begins on the Dream Lake Trail a short way south (left) from Bear Lake. You will see some nice views of Longs Peak and Glacier Gorge framed by aspen on the way to Nymph Lake, but even better views are at Nymph and beyond. Nymph Lake offers a perspective of Hallett Peak and Flattop Mountain different from Bear Lake's. Water lilies float on Nymph's surface.

Abstract grain patterns on burned and uprooted limber pines along the north shore are worth noting. Interesting trees around the lake frame lovely views of Thatchtop Mountain and Longs Peak. Watch for other interesting views of Longs Peak from the trail between Nymph and Dream Lakes.

The best morning scenes of the hike are at Dream Lake (see cover). At a trail junction a bridge crosses Tyndall Creek; turn right before crossing the bridge. At Dream Lake, 0.1 mile from the bridge, wind-shaped limber pines frame views of Hallett and Flattop.

Return to the bridge across Tyndall Creek and continue up switchbacks through a grand subalpine forest. Breaking into the open, the Lake Haiyaha Trail bends around a ridge with good views of Bear and Nymph Lakes, followed by better views of Longs Peak and Glacier Gorge.

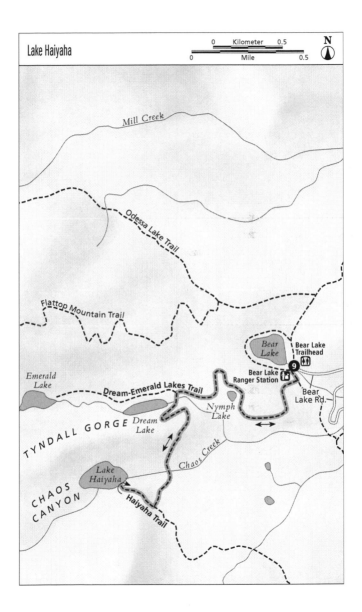

Lake Haiyaha

0   Kilometer   0.5
0   Mile   0.5

N

Mill Creek

Odessa Lake Trail

Flattop Mountain Trail

Bear Lake

Bear Lake Trailhead

9

Bear Lake Ranger Station

Bear Lake Rd.

Emerald Lake

Dream-Emerald Lakes Trail

Nymph Lake

TYNDALL GORGE

Dream Lake

Chaos Creek

Lake Haiyaha

CHAOS CANYON

Haiyaha Trail

A quarter mile before Lake Haiyaha, a connecting trail to Glacier Gorge provides access to many hiking destinations and a longer route back to Bear Lake.

Descend to cross Chaos Creek and bear right through large boulders to Lake Haiyaha, whose Native American name is said to mean "big rocks." The view of Hallett here is less exciting than from the other lakes, but a giant limber pine here is one of the most spectacular examples of this species that I have seen.

Miles and Directions

0.0 About 200 yards west of Bear Lake parking lot, head left on Dream Lake Trail.

0.5 Arrive at Nymph Lake; the trail heads right around the lake.

1.0 Lake Haiyaha Trail cuts left, but detour for 0.1 mile on trail straight ahead for an excellent view of Hallett Peak above Dream Lake, then return to this junction.

1.9 Trail to Glacier Gorge branches to left; take right branch to Lake Haiyaha.

2.1 Arrive at Lake Haiyaha. Turn around.

4.2 Arrive back at Bear Lake parking lot.

10 Emerald Lake

Ascending past glacier-carved lakes, the track ends below dramatic cliffs encircling a timberline tarn.

Start: Bear Lake parking area
Hiking time: 3 hours
Distance: 3.6 miles out-and-back
Difficulty: Easy
Trail surface: Asphalt to dirt
Best season: Summer
Other trail users: Human foot traffic only
Canine compatibility: Dogs are prohibited
Fees and permits: No fees besides park entrance fee
Trail contacts: Rocky Mountain National Park Backcountry Office, 1000 US Hwy 36, Estes Park; (970) 586-1242; www.nps.gov/romo

Maps: Trails Illustrated Rocky Mountain National Park; USGS McHenrys Peak
Highlights: Views of Hallett Peak, Flattop Mountain, and Longs Peak with pond lilies at Nymph Lake, limber pines framing Hallett and Flattop at Dream Lake, Emerald Lake
Wildlife: Mule deer, chipmunk, golden-mantled ground squirrel, gray jay, Clark's nutcracker
Bear Lake Trailhead elevation: 9,475 feet
Dream Lake elevation: 9,900 feet
Emerald Lake elevation: 10,080 feet

Finding the trailhead: Bear Lake is at the end of 9-mile-long Bear Lake Road, which begins near the Beaver Meadows entrance (US 36) of Rocky Mountain National Park (US 36). GPS: N40 18.698' / W105 38.674'

The Hike

Because this trail gives hikers a great deal of spectacular scenery with relatively little effort, it is the most crowded path in Rocky Mountain National Park. Avoid crowds and see the trail at its best by starting to hike before sunrise. Starting early will provide the most dramatic light on the peaks and probably little wind. You also will meet more animals along the trail. The uphill hiking temperature will be cool. And trailhead parking is no problem!

Even by flashlight beam, signs marking the trail to Nymph and Dream Lakes are easy to follow. If you start at the ideal time, it will be too dark for photos at Nymph Lake when you arrive, but you can catch it on the way back.

On your return, use trees on the east shore to frame a photo of Hallett Peak, Flattop Mountain, and the lily pads on the lake surface. Perhaps the trees on the shore will still be in shadow and can be made a silhouette in front of the brightly lit peaks. Be sure to take your light reading off the brightest part of the picture, probably the sky.

Use the same principle to shoot Longs Peak from the trail on the north side of the lake. Just as the trail bends around Nymph's north edge, watch for upended tree roots and burned limber pine trunks, which make grand subjects for close-up abstract photos. Along the trail, the slopes above Nymph Lake are good spots for wildflower photography, as they are somewhat sheltered from wind.

At the Lake Haiyaha Trail junction, keep to the right toward Dream Lake. The lake is the ideal place to be at sunrise, when alpenglow spreads rich colors of changing hues across the faces of Hallett Peak (on the left) and Flattop Mountain. Include the dark, wind-twisted forms of limber pines or companion hikers in the foreground, below the sharp spires of Flattop. The mountain's name may seem perverse, but viewpoint is everything. From a distance, it really is flat and dull-looking. From this trail, the glacier-carved flank is the last word in drama.

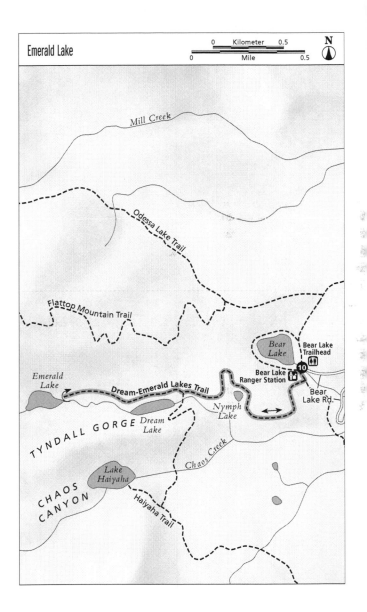

Emerald Lake

Try to use divisions of light and dark within your view of Dream Lake to divide the picture vertically into thirds, and avoid making the surface of the lake a line that cuts the picture in half.

Continue 0.7 mile to Emerald Lake. Watch for views of Tyndall Creek tumbling over bedrock accented by clumps of wildflowers below Flattop.

Miles and Directions

0.0   About 200 yards west of Bear Lake parking lot, head left for Dream Lake.

0.5   Arrive at Nymph Lake.

1.0   Trail to Lake Haiyaha cuts left; continue straight to Dream Lake.

1.1   Arrive Dream Lake; follow lakeshore to right.

1.8   Arrive at Emerald Lake. Turn around to retrace your steps.

3.6   Arrive back at Bear Lake parking lot.

11 Ouzel Falls

Rarely removed from falling water music, this wilderness walk passes through enclosing woods to plummeting falls.

Start: Wild Basin Trailhead
Hiking time: 5 hours
Distance: 5.4 miles out-and-back
Difficulty: Moderately easy
Trail surface: Dirt
Best season: Summer
Other trail users: Equestrians
Canine compatibility: Dogs are prohibited
Fees and permits: No fee besides park entrance fee
Trail contacts: Rocky Mountain National Park Backcountry Office, 1000 US Hwy 36, Estes Park; (970) 586-1242; www.nps.gov/romo

Maps: Trails Illustrated Rocky Mountain National Park; USGS Allenspark
Highlights: Abundant wildflowers, noisy white-water stream, Calypso Cascades, regrowth after 1978 forest fire, Ouzel Falls
Wildlife: Mule deer, red squirrel, chipmunk, yellow-bellied marmot, golden-mantled ground squirrel, water ouzel
Wild Basin Trailhead elevation: 8,500 feet
Calypso Cascades elevation: 9,200 feet
Ouzel Falls elevation: 9,450 feet

Finding the trailhead: Follow CO 7 more than 11 miles south of Estes Park to a well-marked road into Wild Basin (about 2 miles are unpaved and narrow). GPS: N40 12.513' / W105 33.658'

The Hike

Although dawn or earlier is usually the best time to start hiking in Rocky Mountain National Park, this painful practice is unnecessary for a hike to Ouzel Falls, which does not exhibit significant mountain views.

The low, bright light of early morning that illuminates mountain vistas so dramatically is not the best light for viewing shady streamside vistas along the trail to Wild Basin's most popular hiking destination. Sunny skies pour too much light on raging white streams, making so much contrast between water and woods that it is very difficult for your eyes to perceive the whole scene at once. Toward midday the sun will be higher in the sky and often dimmed by clouds, casting an even light by which it is easier to appreciate the wonders of Wild Basin forests.

The lower light level under cloudy skies also permits photographers to steady their cameras on tripods, rocks, or bridge railings to use a slow shutter speed ($\frac{1}{15}$ or $\frac{1}{8}$ second). This slow speed allows moving water to flow into fuzziness while surrounding solid objects remain still during the opening of the camera shutter.

The Wild Basin trails are rich in wildflower species. Watch in particular (in early July) for small pink calypso orchids at trailside near Calypso Cascades. A shaft of sun may penetrate the shade to spotlight one of these orchids.

The burned area beyond Calypso Cascades exhibits the lush green of shrubs and flowers that grew up after forest shade was removed. You are likely to see deer here, as well as marmots and ground squirrels. Appropriately, fireweed is very abundant, but deer often eat its bright magenta blossoms, disappointing hikers who expect to enjoy masses of color. The colors of flowers, leaves, and burned wood blend more pleasingly under overcast rather than sunny skies.

At the bridge over Ouzel Creek below Ouzel Falls (reconstructed after a 2013 flood), leave the main trail to climb along the left bank to the base of the falls. Here you may find the falls graced by the presence of colorful wildflowers.

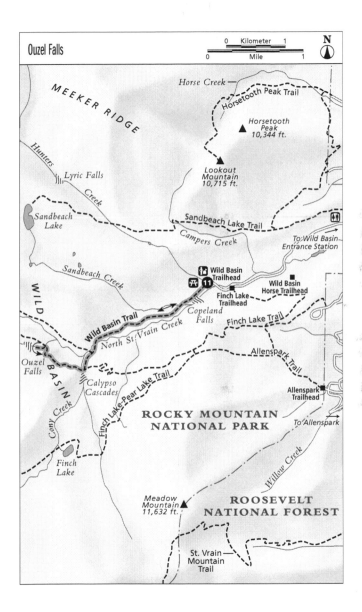

Ouzel Falls is named for a dull gray bird that is a bit smaller than a robin and shaped like a wren. Ouzels also are called dippers because they fly from under the water to land on a rock and perform an entertaining bobbing dance. They stay in the water or just above it rather than flying over the land. You are likely to see ouzels along any of Wild Basin's streams.

Miles and Directions

0.0 From south side of the Wild Basin Trailhead parking lot cross bridge onto the Wild Basin Trail.

1.8 Arrive at Calypso Cascades. (Trail from Allenspark Trailhead comes in from left.) Follow bridges and trail to right toward Ouzel Falls.

2.7 Arrive at bridge across Ouzel Creek. Ouzel Falls is visible to left, but the view obtained by climbing up to the base of the falls definitely is worth the effort.

5.4 Arrive back at Wild Basin Trailhead.

12 Allenspark Trail to Calypso Cascades

These cascades display lovely pink Calypso orchids in mid-summer. Forest fire has opened views of high peaks above Wild Basin.

Start: Allenspark Trailhead
Hiking time: 5 hours
Distance: 6.2 miles out-and-back
Difficulty: Moderately easy
Trail surface: Dirt
Best season: Summer
Other trail users: Equestrians
Canine compatibility: Dogs are prohibited.
Fees and permits: None
Trail contacts: Rocky Mountain National Park Backcountry Office, 1000 US Hwy 36, Estes Park; (970) 586-1242; www.nps.gov/romo

Maps: Trails Illustrated Rocky Mountain National Park; USGS Allenspark
Highlights: Forest fire of 1978, interesting trail building, views of Longs Peak, Calypso Cascades
Wildlife: Red squirrel, chipmunk, golden-mantled ground squirrel, mountain chickadee, Steller's jay, gray jay, mule deer
Allenspark Trailhead elevation: 8,520 feet
Calypso Cascades elevation: 9,200 feet

Finding the trailhead: From CO 7, turn south on Business 7 (Washington Street) into the town of Allenspark. Drive 1 block and turn right onto unpaved CR 90. After 0.7 mile, bear left uphill onto South Skinner Road. After 0.5 mile, turn right onto Meadow Mountain Drive and continue a short distance to the Allenspark Trail parking area on the right. GPS: N40 09.924' / W105 11.180'

The Hike

Calypso Cascades is a popular destination in Rocky Mountain National Park, but by starting at the Allenspark

Trailhead, the hike to the cascades is free from the bustle of crowds until you reach the destination. The trail offers interesting scenery opened by a 1978 forest fire.

Whereas hiking the main trail in Wild Basin is a streamside experience, hiking Allenspark Trail is a study of the effect of forest fire. In 1978 a lightning-generated fire swept through Wild Basin. A good deal of the burning occurred on the side of Meadow Mountain along which this trail runs. The burn opened up the old forest and created spectacular views of Longs Peak, Pagoda Mountain, Chiefshead, and the mountains at the head of Wild Basin.

These views appear beyond the first junction along the Allenspark Trail. To take the best route to Calypso Cascades go left at this junction. The views are lovely, but the openness makes this hike seem rather warm and steep unless you begin early in the day, when morning light is most lovely on the incredible views to the northwest.

Trailside vegetation has changed since the forest fire. Now, large areas of the trail are lined with pioneering shrubs and wildflowers that attract deer and elk. Small, new stands of aspen also have appeared, utilizing the sunny hillside habitats and paving the way for the next generation of plants to take root.

The fire did more than damage the forest vegetation, however. Burning into the soil itself and denuding the forest floor, it caused great erosion along the trail, especially near Confusion Junction where the Finch Lake and Allenspark Trails divide. Just beyond the junction, some extreme trail building measures hold the erosion at bay. Along one stretch of trail, where log walls seem to shore up a whole mountainside, a spectacular view of Longs Peak is visible. Not far beyond, the trail enters undisturbed primeval forest typical of

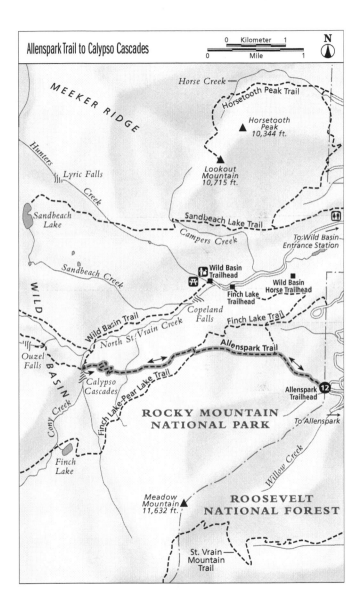

Allenspark Trail to Calypso Cascades

N

| 0 | Kilometer | 1 |
| 0 | Mile | 1 |

Horse Creek

MEEKER RIDGE

Horsetooth Peak Trail

Hunters

Lyric Falls

Horsetooth Peak
10,344 ft.

Lookout
Mountain
10,715 ft.

Creek

*Sandbeach
Lake*

Sandbeach Lake Trail

Campers Creek

To Wild Basin
Entrance Station

Sandbeach Creek

WILD

Wild Basin
Trailhead

Wild Basin
Horse Trailhead

Finch Lake
Trailhead

*Copeland
Falls*

Finch Lake Trail

Wild Basin Trail

*Ouzel
Falls*

BASIN

North St. Vrain Creek

Allenspark Trail

*Calypso
Cascades*

Cony Creek

Finch Lake–Pear Lake Trail

Allenspark
Trailhead

12

To Allenspark

ROCKY MOUNTAIN
NATIONAL PARK

*Finch
Lake*

Willow Creek

Meadow
Mountain
11,632 ft.

ROOSEVELT
NATIONAL FOREST

St. Vrain
Mountain
Trail

much of Wild Basin. The contrast is quite stunning, and it's cool and fragrant. An elaborate bridge with stone pavement on each side crosses an unnamed creek before you descend several switchbacks to the junction with the main Wild Basin Trail at Calypso Cascades.

Miles and Directions

0.0   Start at Allenspark Trailhead.

0.7   Trail drops right; continue ascending Allenspark Trail to left.

1.6   Reach aptly named Confusion Junction; continue straight across Finch Lake Trail.

3.1   Arrive at Calypso Cascades. Turn around to retrace your steps.

6.2   Arrive back at Allenspark Trailhead.

13 Fall River Road

This one-lane byway drops through three life zones and is closed to vehicles during much of the year, when it makes an excellent route for hikers.

Start: Fall River Pass
Hiking time: About 8 hours
Distance: 9.0-mile shuttle (5.2-mile out-and-back to Chasm Falls)
Difficulty: Moderately easy
Trail surface: Dirt
Best season: Early summer
Other trail users: Bicycles in early spring through late fall; cars after snow is removed at top of the road
Canine compatibility: Dogs are permitted to hike the road after Trail Ridge opens in late May, as indicated by signs
Fees and permits: No fee besides park entrance fee

Trail contacts: Rocky Mountain National Park Backcountry Office; 1000 US Hwy 36, Estes Park; (970) 586-1242; www.nps.gov/romo
Maps: Trails Illustrated Rocky Mountain National Park; USGS Fall River Pass and Trail Ridge
Highlights: Chasm Falls, avalanche site
Wildlife: Mule deer, elk
West Alluvial Fan parking lot elevation: 8,250 feet
Chasm Falls elevation: 9,060 feet
Fall River Pass elevation: 11,796 feet

Finding the trailhead: In spring, when Trail Ridge Road reopens (probably sometime in late May), hikers can leave one car at Fall River Pass on Trail Ridge Road and another near the bottom of Old Fall River Road at the West Alluvial Fan parking area, or closer, in Endovalley Picnic Area or in roadside turnouts east of Old Fall River Road.

From the park's Fall River entrance, follow US 34 for 2.1 miles to the Fall River Road turnoff. The West Alluvial Fan parking area is

0.8 mile along Fall River Road (past the first parking area labeled "Alluvial Fan") 1.2 miles east of the base of Old Fall River Road. GPS: N40 24.62' / W105 38.27'. The base of Old Fall River Road is GPS N40 24.85' / W105 39.31'. Fall River Pass on Trail Ridge Road is GPS N40 24.62' / W105 45.26'.

The Hike

Old Fall River Road was the first motorized route to transect Rocky Mountain National Park, opening in 1920. Many centuries earlier, however, Arapaho travelers called this the Dog Trail because their dogs pulled travois bearing the Native Americans' burdens over this route to the other side of the mountains.

Today, from the first Saturday in April (when there is access to the bottom of the road) until road crews reopen Old Fall River Road after winter closure (probably early July), it is one of the few places in this national park where hikers can re-create this human-canine partnership with dog packs. To preserve this opportunity for everyone, hikers absolutely must keep their dogs leashed according to park regulations.

In winter, Chasm Falls, a 2.6-mile walk along closed paved and unpaved roads, is a good safe hike. The nearest winter trailhead is 1.2 miles from the old road at the West Alluvial Fan parking lot. Exactly when winter ends is hard to determine. Absence of road closure may enable you to park closer (in small roadside parking spots) in spring and early summer.

This is one of the park's best areas to see elk, as indicated by the heavy black scarring of aspen trunks along the paved road that runs along the Fall River valley floor. Elk strip off the bark for winter food.

The right turn up unpaved Old Fall River Road is obvious. From the start of the unpaved road it is another 1.4 miles

Fall River Road

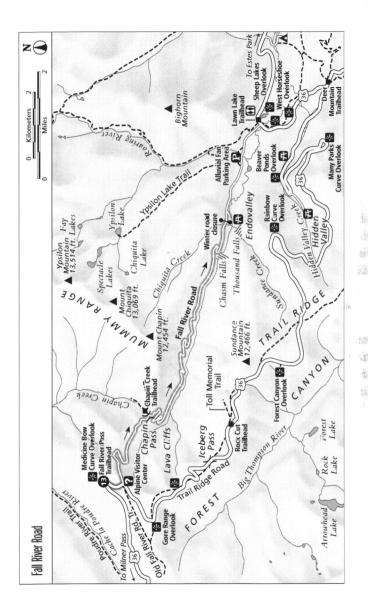

to Chasm Falls, where potholes at the base of the falls were scoured thousands of years ago by glacial meltwater dropping through ice cracks and swirling rocks. Fall River continues the same process at the base of the 25-foot falls. Be very careful of steep, slick surfaces when you are near the falls.

Hikers along Old Fall River Road may notice results of September 2013 flooding, which wiped out sections of the road. This damage closed the road for repair during 2014.

In winter of 1985-86, a major avalanche snapped off many large trees, visible in a jumbled mass as you look left (north) up the slope of Mount Chapin 5.3 miles down from Fall River Pass (3.7 miles from the bottom of the unpaved road). This avalanche had not run for many decades. No one knows when or where the next unpleasant surprise may roar across the road, but particular care by winter hikers who venture up the road in winter is necessary after heavy snows. Avalanche danger likely increases with altitude as far as Chapin Pass Trailhead, 8 miles from the Alluvial Fan.

Above Chasm Falls, watch for bighorn sheep on rock outcrops north of the road. Elk often appear on the road itself and across the valley on the side of Sundance Mountain.

After Trail Ridge Road reopens, probably in late May, hikers have access to Fall River Pass and can hike downhill all the way to Horseshoe Park. This is a great hike in June, passing through all of the national park's life zones, but requires arranging transportation at both ends of Old Fall River Road.

Miles and Directions

0.0 Start at Fall River Pass where Old Fall River Road descends north (left) of the Fall River Pass Store.

9.0 Arrive at base of the road in the upper reaches of Horseshoe Park.

14 Gem Lake

This trail winds amid uncounted granite monoliths to a gem's setting on the east end of Lumpy Ridge.

Start: Gem Lake Trailhead
Hiking time: 3 hours
Distance: 3.4 miles out-and-back
Difficulty: Moderately easy
Trail surface: Dirt
Best season: Spring
Other trail users: Equestrians
Canine compatibility: Dogs are prohibited
Fees and permits: No fees besides park entrance fee
Trail contacts: Rocky Mountain National Park Backcountry Office, 1000 US Hwy 36, Estes Park;

(970) 586-1242; www.nps.gov/romo
Maps: Trails Illustrated Rocky Mountain National Park; USGS Glen Haven and Estes Park
Highlights: Unique rock formations, views of Longs Peak above Estes Valley, Gem Lake
Wildlife: Mule deer, Richardson and golden-mantled ground squirrel, white-throated swift
Twin Owls Trailhead elevation: 7,740 feet
Gem Lake elevation: 8,830 feet

Finding the trailhead: From downtown Estes Park, drive north on MacGregor Avenue (which becomes Devils Gulch Road) about 2 miles to a well-marked left turn leading to the Gem Lake and Lumpy Ridge trailheads. GPS: N40 23.57' / W105 30.75'

The Hike

Popular throughout the year, Gem Lake is a particularly good hike for folks eager to experience spring on the trail. In Rocky Mountain National Park, the Gem Lake Trail sees spring first. Here is the place to observe pasqueflowers pushing their purple tulip heads through the forest duff. Watch for bitterbrush blooming first near the surface of rocks that

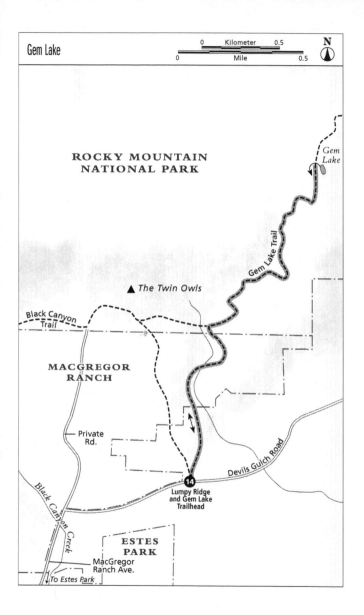

are solar collectors, radiating heat to create early spring before the season arrives for most other plants.

Even the most unimaginative of hikers can see a pair of owls in the two huge granite pillars that rise above the trailhead on Lumpy Ridge. Equally obvious is Paul Bunyan's Boot about halfway to Gem Lake. Wind and mildly acidic rain have sculpted countless other abstract monoliths along the trail into formations fascinating to both romantic and prosaic minds. It is a natural playground for children, but parents need to supervise and warn kids to avoid falls from slick rocks.

Gem Lake is a small jewel in a big setting. Actually a large (0.2 acre) pothole in the granite, it has no inlet or outlet and averages a foot deep. Its beauty, therefore, is more subtle than that of the grand alpine lakes higher in the park. Notice the abstract color patterns of lichens at the base of the cliffs on the north shore. Limber pines frame the distant peaks.

Weathering of rocks atop the cliff above the lake has created remarkable patterns of potholes. The easiest way to reach these is to clamber very carefully up the less steep slope around the corner of the rock bulwark on the north side of the lake.

Climbing to the top of the cliff may also bring you closer to white-throated swifts, birds that look like cigars with swept-back wings. They dart at very high speeds over the water in pursuit of flying insects.

Miles and Directions

0.0 Start at the Gem Lake Trailhead, the right of two trails leaving from the starting point.

1.7 Arrive at Gem Lake. Turn around to retrace your route.

3.4 Arrive back at Gem Lake Trailhead.

15 Bridal Veil Falls

Meadows and aspen groves surround the way to a falls easy to imagine from its name.

Start: Cow Creek Trailhead
Hiking time: 4 hours
Distance: 6.0 miles out-and-back
Difficulty: Moderately easy
Trail surface: Dirt
Best season: Fall
Other trail users: Equestrians as far as a hitch rail below the falls
Canine compatibility: Dogs are prohibited
Fees and permits: No fees besides park entrance fee

Trail contacts: Rocky Mountain National Park Backcountry Office, 1000 US Hwy 36, Estes Park; (970) 586-1242; www. nps.gov/romo
Maps: Trails Illustrated Rocky Mountain National Park; USGS Estes Park
Highlights: Aspen-lined Cow Creek, Bridal Veil Falls
Wildlife: Elk, mule deer
Cow Creek Trailhead elevation: 7,840 feet
Bridal Veil Falls elevation: 8,900 feet

Finding the trailhead: From downtown Estes Park, follow Devils Gulch Road 3.9 miles to McGraw Ranch Road. Turn left and drive 2.3 miles to the Cow Creek Trailhead at the end of this unpaved road. Parking is only permitted in the parking area at the trailhead. Do not park along the road beyond the ranch boundary. GPS: N40 24.88' / W105 30.06'

The Hike

Cow Creek presumably was named for the livestock at McGraw Ranch, established in 1874. The cattle were gone long before McGraw Ranch became part of Rocky Mountain National Park in 1988. There were many cows along Cow Creek nonetheless—cow elk and admiring bulls, of course.

You have an excellent chance of spotting elk along Cow Creek on the way to Bridal Veil Falls, particularly in winter, so if you have a telephoto lens and tripod, haul them along. The extra effort could yield a prizewinning photo.

The trail to the falls is relatively easy. The path meanders west from the trailhead, usually staying in the open meadows that are vital sources of food for elk. Usually free of winter snow, the path can be rather warm in the summer. Using sunscreen is a good idea throughout the year.

Hikers need not be particularly observant to see that the elk do not feed only on the grass. They also eat willows and streamside shrubs. The black scars on aspen bark are particularly obvious signs of elk dining. The double vertical scars show where elk use their lower incisors to strip bark from the trees. Light-colored wood indicates more recent feeding; it eventually turns black. The rough black scars contrasting with the smooth, nearly white aspen bark can create some interesting patterns for close-up photography.

Beavers also feed on the aspen and use it extensively to construct dams and lodges. Many beaver ponds slow the flow of Cow Creek, providing excellent opportunities in fall for reflection photos of aspen gold.

Actually spotting the beavers themselves will be a matter of luck. They are in significant danger from predators when they are out of the water, and they tend to do most of their cutting at night. The beavers are most active in summer and fall, when they store aspen and willow branches and trunks under the surface of the water. After winter freezes the surface, they reach their stores by an underwater entrance from their den or lodge.

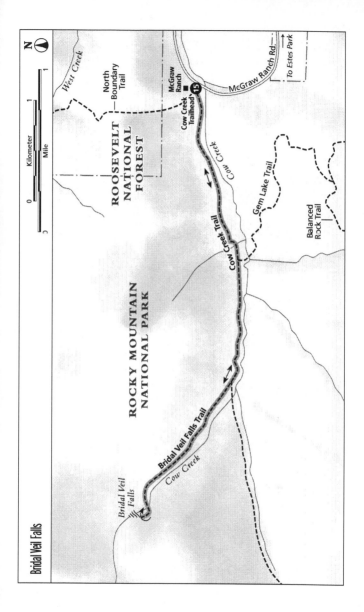

Bridal Veil Falls

Bridal Veil Falls is one of the prettiest in the park. It is especially spectacular in spring, when the torrent of melting snow rushes over the falls with so much force that the water gushes back into the air from the pool below the falls. In winter, the more subtle beauties of frozen splashes and streamside ice patterns create a lovely setting.

Miles and Directions

0.0 Start at Cow Creek Trailhead.

0.1 North Boundary Trail cuts steeply up to right; continue straight along Cow Creek.

1.1 Bridal Veil Falls Trail branches to right along Cow Creek, departing from Cow Creek Trail, which swings away from its namesake.

3.0 Arrive at Bridal Veil Falls. Turn around to return.

6.0 Arrive back at Cow Creek Trailhead.

16 West Creek Falls

Trudging steeply uphill at its beginning, this route drops almost as steeply before it moderates to a pleasant grade to secluded falls.

Start: Cow Creek Trailhead
Hiking time: 3 hours
Distance: 4.0 miles out-and-back
Difficulty: Moderate
Trail surface: Dirt
Best season: Summer
Other trail users: Equestrians
Canine compatibility: Dogs are prohibited
Fees and permits: No fee besides park entrance fee
Trail contacts: Rocky Mountain National Park Backcountry Office, 1000 US Hwy 36, Estes Park;

(970) 586-1242; www.nps.gov/romo
Maps: Trails Illustrated Rocky Mountain National Park; USGS Glen Haven and Estes Park
Highlights: McGraw Ranch, West Creek Falls
Wildlife: Mule deer, elk, red squirrel
Cow Creek Trailhead elevation: 7,840 feet
West Creek Falls elevation: 8,160 feet
High point: 8,440 feet

Finding the trailhead: From downtown Estes Park, follow Devils Gulch Road 3.9 miles to McGraw Ranch Road. Turn left and drive 2.3 miles to the Cow Creek Trailhead at the end of this unpaved road. Parking is only permitted in the parking area at the trailhead. Do not park along the road beyond the ranch boundary. GPS: N40 24.88' / W104 30.06'

The Hike

McGraw Ranch, one of the oldest in this area, was established in 1874. Cow Creek gained its name soon after, presumably from the stock on the ranch. Various architectural

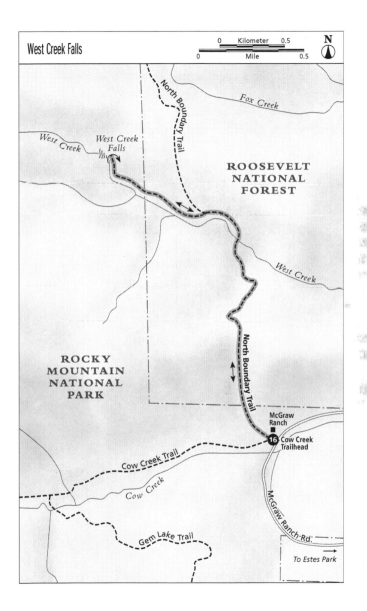

West Creek Falls

West Creek

West Creek Falls

North Boundary Trail

Fox Creek

ROOSEVELT
NATIONAL
FOREST

West Creek

North Boundary Trail

ROCKY
MOUNTAIN
NATIONAL
PARK

McGraw
Ranch

16 Cow Creek
Trailhead

Cow Creek Trail

Cow Creek

McGraw Ranch Rd.

Gem Lake Trail

To Estes Park

Kilometer

Mile

N

details of the ranch structures make good photo subjects and backgrounds for portraits.

Even a century ago it was obvious that catering to tourists made more economic sense than catering to cows. McGraw Ranch enabled many guests to experience the beauty of its out-of-the-way valley.

The back of a horse was the favored vantage point of these guests. Just west of the ranch buildings, the North Boundary Trail to West Creek Falls heads right up a ridge, the route of guests content to let horses do the puffing and panting.

From the low point on the ridge between West and Cow Creeks, the trail weaves back and forth steeply down through a Douglas-fir forest to West Creek. Across the creek, head left (west) at a trail intersection and walk a gentle grade along the bank to West Creek Falls. In this peaceful setting of a rocky amphitheater, the creek descends in two tiers.

Miles and Directions

0.0 Start at Cow Creek Trailhead at McGraw Ranch.

0.1 Cut sharply right up North Boundary Trail.

1.4 Cross West Creek, where trail to right eventually circles back to ranch, then head left on trail up West Creek.

2.0 Arrive at West Creek Falls.

4.0 Arrive back at Cow Creek Trailhead.

17 Timberline Pass

Undulating entirely above the trees, this track used by ancient Utes amid jagged peaks descends a bit to a giant pile of rocks surrounded by alpine tundra.

Start: Ute Crossing
Hiking time: 3 hours
Distance: 4.0 miles out-and-back
Difficulty: Moderately easy
Trail surface: Rocks and dirt
Best season: Midsummer
Other trail users: Human foot traffic only
Canine compatibility: Dogs are prohibited
Fees and permits: No fees besides park entrance fee
Trail contacts: Rocky Mountain National Park Backcountry Office, 1000 US Hwy 36, Estes Park;

(970) 586-1242; www.nps.gov/romo
Maps: Trails Illustrated Rocky Mountain National Park; USGS Trail Ridge and McHenrys Peak
Highlights: Open vistas, various tundra environments with many flower species
Wildlife: Water pipet, horned lark, pika, yellow-bellied marmot, elk
Ute Crossing elevation: 11,440 feet
Timberline Pass elevation: 11,484 feet

Finding the trailhead: Ute Crossing is just above tree line, 2 miles above Rainbow Curve and 0.8 mile downhill from Forest Canyon Overlook. There is additional parking a short walk up Trail Ridge Road from Ute Crossing. GPS: N40 23.60' / W105 41.72'

The Hike

This is a section of the Old Ute Trail (called the Child's Trail by the Utes), which extends across the Continental Divide from Estes Park to Grand Lake. Trail Ridge Road overlays much of this ancient past.

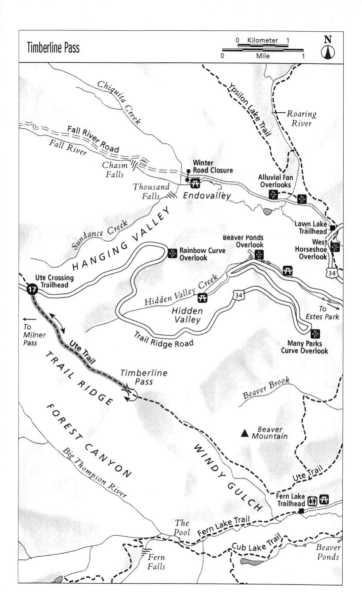

Timberline Pass

0   Kilometer   1
0   Mile   1

N

Chiquita Creek

Ypsilon Lake Trail

Roaring River

Fall River Road

Fall River

Chasm Falls

Thousand Falls

Winter Road Closure

Endovalley

Alluvial Fan Overlooks

Sundance Creek

HANGING VALLEY

Rainbow Curve Overlook

Beaver Ponds Overlook

Lawn Lake Trailhead

West Horseshoe Overlook

34

Ute Crossing Trailhead

17

Hidden Valley Creek

Hidden Valley

34

To Estes Park

To Milner Pass

Ute Trail

TRAIL RIDGE

Trail Ridge Road

Many Parks Curve Overlook

Timberline Pass

FOREST CANYON

Big Thompson River

Beaver Brook

▲ Beaver Mountain

WINDY GULCH

Ute Trail

Fern Lake Trailhead

The Pool

Fern Lake Trail

Cub Lake Trail

Beaver Ponds

Fern Falls

From the Ute Crossing on Trail Ridge Road, a delightful and easy tundra walk passes through most of the tundra plant communities: disturbed areas, snow-accumulated areas, mature meadows, marshes, and krummholtz (wind-distorted trees). A good destination is a tor—a mass of disintegrating, flower-filled bedrock—in Timberline Pass.

As the trail undulates across the tundra south of the road, hikers' eyes naturally turn to the highly glaciated peaks to the south (right) rising near at hand above trackless Forest Canyon and farther away above the Bear Lake area and Glacier Gorge. The flat-topped tower that rises above all others far to the south is Longs Peak, the highest mountain in the national park at 14,259 feet.

Scattered along the trail are more tors that caused this part of Trail Ridge to be called Tombstone Ridge. This ominous name might remind you to retreat to your cars if storm clouds build. There is no protection from lightning along the ridge.

Hike early in the day to avoid storms and reduce wind disruption of flower photography. Because tundra plants have no protection from trampling feet, stay on the path between piled-up rock markers (cairns) as much as possible. When investigating a point of interest away from the path, step on rocks and avoid other hikers' footsteps.

Miles and Directions

0.0 Start at Ute Crossing.

2.0 Arrive at Timberline Pass, marked by large tor (hill of rocks). Turn around to retrace your route.

4.0 Arrive back at Ute Crossing.

18 Toll Memorial

A short, paved path climbs over gentle, terrain well above the trees.

Start: Rock Cut
Hiking time: 2 hours
Distance: 0.8 mile out-and-back
Difficulty: Moderately easy
Trail surface: Asphalt
Best season: Midsummer
Other trail users: Wheelchairs
Canine compatibility: Dogs are prohibited
Fees and permits: No fees besides park entrance fee
Trail contacts: Rocky Mountain National Park Backcountry Office, 1000 US Hwy 36, Estes Park;
(970) 586-1242; www.nps.gov/romo
Maps: Trails Illustrated Rocky Mountain National Park; USGS Trail Ridge
Highlights: Alpine plants, Mushroom Rocks, Toll Memorial peak finder
Wildlife: Yellow-bellied marmot, pika, chipmunk, raven, Clark's nutcracker
Rock Cut Trailhead elevation: 12,110 feet
Toll Memorial elevation: 12,310 feet

Finding the trailhead: Rock Cut Trailhead is well marked along Trail Ridge Road 12.5 miles from the junction of US 34 and US 36. GPS: N40 24.70' / W105 4.80'

The Hike

Rock Cut is the highest trailhead in Rocky Mountain National Park and one of the busiest. Rock blasted from Rock Cut during road construction was used for road buttress across from the trailhead and also dumped nearby on the alpine tundra. The result is a natural–looking but unnaturally abundant accumulation of ideal rock habitat for cute, round-eared rabbit relatives called pika (see back cover). Take care when crossing the road and watch the pika from above along the retaining wall.

Thousands of people walking on embattled tundra plants would damage them significantly. Therefore, in this Tundra Protection Zone, stay on the paved trail.

The best diversity of tundra plants along the trail occurs at the trailhead, the most sheltered place for low-angle, tripod-using, wait-for-the-miserable-wind-to-quit photography of flowers. Typical of this area are some larger tundra species: purple fringe, sky pilot, bistort, and alpine sunflower.

For the first 0.25 mile, the edge of the asphalt is crowded by cushion plants pioneering the wind-scoured rock fields. Pink moss campion predominates, with white alpine sandwort also heroically struggling to bring life to the barren domain of the bitter wind. Watch for patterns of tundra flowers growing amid lines of jagged rocks (felsenmeer) heaved together and thrust up by the freezing and thawing of the ground.

The progress of this effort can be judged a short way up the trail, where an abandoned road dating from the construction of Trail Ridge Road comes in from the left. Quarry rock was transported along this road in the early 1930s. Although the twin ruts of truck tires are still obvious in the shape of the ground, the cushion plants have made equally obvious progress in covering the surface.

The path's beginning steepness distresses many motorists, who drive quickly and easily from oxygen-rich air at low altitude to thin air at high altitude and then attempt this hike. After the grade flattens, a spur path takes hikers to

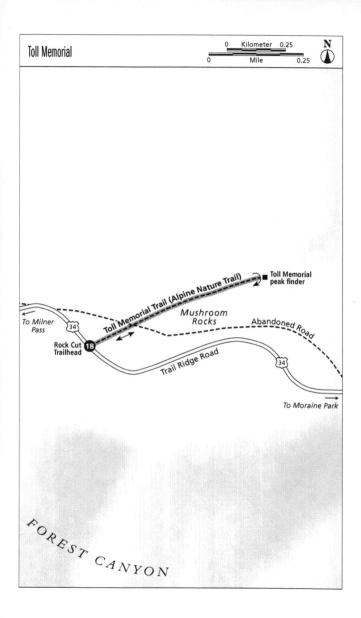

Mushroom Rocks, caprock formations unusual in this park. White feldspar that fractures easily into plates makes up most of the rock below caps of hard schist, more resistant to wind and temperature erosion.

Stark color contrast and mushroom shapes make the rocks very photogenic. Less obvious is the pattern of cushion plants standing out against an unusual background of white rock chips along the trail west of Mushroom Rocks.

The last half of the trail is relatively flat until the last scramble up a rock outcrop to the peak finder that memorializes Roger Toll, the third park superintendent, who envisioned the building of Trail Ridge Road. The easier grade relieves the lungs, but does not help skin chilled by wind and low temperature and scorched by UV radiation. Appropriate clothing and sunscreen greatly enhance your enjoyment of the high-altitude tundra.

Miles and Directions

0.0 Start at Rock Cut Trailhead on north side of Trail Ridge Road.

0.25 Spur path to right leads to Mushroom Rocks.

0.4 Reach Toll Memorial peak finder by scrambling to the top of rocks.

0.8 Arrive back at Rock Cut Trailhead.

19 Fall River Pass to Milner Pass

A track across alpine tundra descends amid expansive views of the Never Summer Range.

Start: Fall River Pass
Hiking time: 3 hours
Distance: 4.0-mile shuttle
Difficulty: Moderately easy
Trail surface: Dirt
Best season: Summer
Other trail users: Human foot traffic only
Canine compatibility: Dogs are prohibited
Fees and permits: No fees besides park entrance fee
Trail contacts: Rocky Mountain National Park Backcountry Office,

1000 US Hwy 36, Estes Park; (970) 586-1242; www.nps.gov/romo
Maps: Trails Illustrated Rocky Mountain National Park; USGS Fall River Pass
Highlights: Alpine tundra, good views of Never Summer Range
Wildlife: Mule deer, elk, ptarmigan, white-crowned sparrow
Fall River Pass elevation: 11,796 feet
Milner Pass elevation: 10,750 feet

Finding the trailhead: Fall River Pass is located along Trail Ridge Road about midway between Estes Park and Grand Lake. Milner Pass is 4.2 miles west of Fall River Pass on Trail Ridge Road. GPS: N40 26.49' / W105 45.26' (Fall River Pass); N40 25.22' / W105 48.70' (Milner Pass)

The Hike

One of the easiest and most pleasant trails in Rocky Mountain National Park is relatively uncrowded because of logistical complications in arranging transportation at both ends of the trail. All downhill, a stroll along the 1918–32 road route from Fall River Pass to Milner Pass follows a very easy grade. If you cannot work out a car shuttle to put wheels on both ends of the trail, the way back up to Fall River Pass from midway down at Forest Canyon Pass is not terribly steep.

Abandoned when the present route of Trail Ridge Road was opened, the old route is an obvious path beginning across the road from the parking lot at Fall River Pass. Revegetation is still in its initial stage as the tundra cushion plants, primarily moss campion, pioneer the barren gravel once traveled by Model Ts. This is one of the best places in the national park to view the process of plant succession. The campion traps bits of windblown dirt under its many-branched stem, hoarding the soil until this reservoir of dirt can support plants less hardy than the pioneer campion. The campion shelters their seeds from fierce wind and provides food and moisture. Then the new plants establish themselves and crowd out the campion.

The old road offers a very fine view south to the Never Summer Range. The rusty red of the distant peaks accents a foreground of tundra flowers. Below Forest Canyon Pass, clumps of wind-abused Engelmann spruce provide a dramatic foreground for the rugged Never Summer Range.

Soon hikers traverse a forest where the same spruce species grows straight and tall. Bogs below melting snowbanks and occasional avalanche runs open the woods, giving light to masses of Indian paintbrush and other subalpine flowers. Where deep woods prevail, Jacob's ladder, with its ladderlike leaves and pale blue flowers, provides the ground cover.

A sign at a trail junction indicates that continuing straight takes hikers to a climb up Mount Ida. Make a sharp right turn to drop through gentle switchbacks to the Continental Divide at Milner Pass.

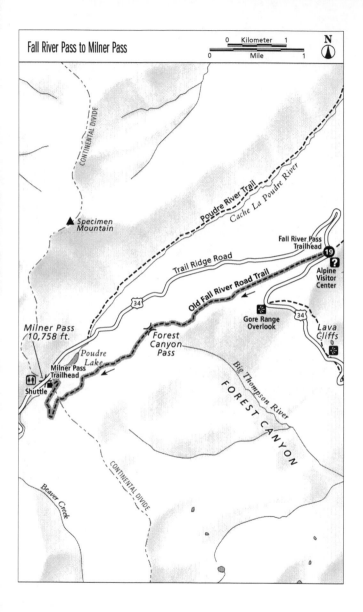

Fall River Pass to Milner Pass

N

0 Kilometer 1
0 Mile 1

CONTINENTAL DIVIDE

Poudre River Trail

Cache La Poudre River

Specimen Mountain

Fall River Pass Trailhead

19

Alpine Visitor Center

Trail Ridge Road

Old Fall River Road Trail

34

Gore Range Overlook

34

Lava Cliffs

Milner Pass 10,758 ft.

Poudre Lake

Forest Canyon Pass

Milner Pass Trailhead

Shuttle

Big Thompson River

FOREST CANYON

CONTINENTAL DIVIDE

Beaver Creek

Miles and Directions

0.0 Start across Trail Ridge Road from entrance to Fall River Pass parking lot.

2.5 The route levels in Forest Canyon Pass.

4.0 Arrive at Milner Pass. Turn around to retrace your steps.

8.0 Arrive back at Fall River Pass parking lot.

20 Lulu City

A ramble along the peaceful headwaters of the Colorado River passes faint ruins of faint mining dreams set in pastoral majesty.

Start: Colorado River Trailhead
Hiking time: 7 hours
Distance: 7.4 miles out-and-back
Difficulty: Moderately easy
Trail surface: Dirt
Best season: Summer
Other trail users: Equestrians
Canine compatibility: Dogs are prohibited
Fees and permits: No fees besides park entrance fee
Trail contacts: Rocky Mountain National Park Backcountry Office, 1000 US Hwy 36, Estes Park;

(970) 586-1242; www.nps.gov/romo
Maps: Trails Illustrated Rocky Mountain National Park; USGS Fall River Pass
Highlights: Shipler Mine, Lulu City
Wildlife: Elk, mule deer, gray jay, red squirrel
Colorado River Trailhead elevation: 9,010 feet
Lulu City elevation: 9,360 feet

Finding the trailhead: The Colorado River Trailhead is on the west side of Trail Ridge Road, 9.6 miles north of the Grand Lake entrance to Rocky Mountain National Park and 10.7 miles southwest of Fall River Pass. GPS: N40 24.06' / W105 50.92'

The Hike

Lulu City was never a city, and it was never a lulu. Lulu City was a vain hope that silver deposits in the Never Summer Range would be rich enough to exploit profitably. The streets laid out on paper in 1880 never passed more than the few buildings it took to serve 50 to 200 residents until the community's complete abandonment by 1884. These buildings are gone, and the few remaining logs and stone foundations and rusting bits of mining machinery are not obvious.

Distracted by the rich scenery, hikers often give no thought to the riches sought by Lulu City founders and residents. Even history enthusiasts usually are more impressed by the unbankable riches of wildflower color and jagged, snow-accented skyline than by the hopes of silver miners.

At 0.6 mile from the trailhead is the site of the old Phantom Valley guest ranch, where a trail to Red Mountain splits left from the trail to Lulu City and La Poudre Pass. The way to Lulu City continues fairly level along the Colorado River. Willows and other floodplain plants line the trail, and the workings of beavers are obvious. Human workings also appear in an 1880s mine site to the right of the trail beyond the split.

Shipler Mine, at 2.5 miles, preceded Lulu City and lasted until 1914. It likely was no more successful at producing silver, but Joe Shipler loved the land and hung on despite lack of riches, a common story even today in Grand County. He built his first sod-roofed cabin in 1876 and over the years managed to peck 100 yards into the granite of Shipler Mountain. Very lucky hikers may see mountain sheep amid the rubble of Shipler's mining efforts. (Stay out of all old mines; they are not safe.)

Passing on a level grade beyond the cabins, the trail follows a stage road that ran to Lulu City before heading northwest over Thunder Pass to Walden, Colorado. When at last the trail climbs above the valley floor, the shade of subalpine forest through which you walk is welcome. The trail forks at a junction 3.5 miles from the trailhead. The

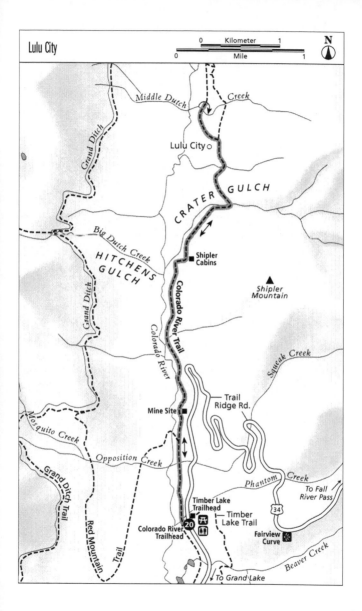

Lulu City

0   Kilometer   1
0   Mile   1

N

Middle Dutch   *Creek*

Lulu City○

CRATER GULCH

Grand Ditch

Big Dutch Creek

HITCHENS
GULCH

■ Shipler Cabins

▲ *Shipler
Mountain*

Grand Ditch

Colorado River Trail

Colorado River

Squeak Creek

■ Mine Site

Trail
Ridge Rd.

Mosquito Creek

Opposition Creek

Phantom Creek

To Fall
River Pass

Grand Ditch Trail

Red Mountain
Trail

34

Timber Lake
Trailhead

Colorado River
Trailhead   20

Timber
Lake Trail

Fairview
Curve

Beaver Creek

↙ To Grand Lake

right-hand fork goes to the eroded volcanic rock of Little Yellowstone Canyon and La Poudre Pass. The left-hand fork heads back downhill through switchbacks for about 0.2 mile to the meadow that contained Lulu City. The Thunder Pass Trail continues through the meadow and past a steep connecting trail up to the La Poudre Pass Trail.

Miles and Directions

0.0 Start at Colorado River Trailhead.

2.5 Shipler Mine is not particularly obvious, which is just as well; mine workings are dangerous.

3.5 The trail splits; take left fork downhill.

3.7 Arrive at Lulu City site. Turn around to retrace your steps.

7.4 Arrive back at Colorado River Trailhead.

21 Big Meadows

A lush trail passes tumbledown historic structures.

Start: Green Mountain Trailhead
Hiking time: 6 hours
Distance: 7.0-mile loop
Difficulty: Easy
Trail surface: Dirt
Best season: Summer
Other trail users: Equestrians
Canine compatibility: Dogs are prohibited
Fees and permits: No fees besides park entrance fee
Trail contacts: Rocky Mountain National Park Backcountry Office, 1000 US Hwy 36, Estes Park;
(970) 586-1242; www.nps.gov/romo
Maps: Trails Illustrated Rocky Mountain National Park; USGS Grand Lake
Highlights: Circle hike, Big Meadows, log building ruins
Wildlife: Mule deer, elk, red squirrel, mountain chickadee
Green Mountain Trailhead elevation: 8,794 feet
Big Meadows elevation: 9,400 feet

Finding the trailhead: The Onahu Creek and Green Mountain trailheads are 0.7 mile apart and are well marked along Trail Ridge Road, about 3 miles north of the Grand Lake entrance to Rocky Mountain National Park and 17 miles southwest of Fall River Pass. GPS: N40 18.97' / W105 50.61' (Onahu Creek Trailhead); GPS: N40 18.45' / W105 50.49' (Green Mountain Trailhead)

The Hike

Some folks in turn-of-the-twentieth-century Grand Lake thought Sam Stone was crazy. Perhaps he would seem less so today, since Colorado has attracted a population with a higher-than-average percentage of eccentrics. In any case, Sam tried to produce hay in marshy Big Meadows, which he hauled by wagon down what now is the Green Mountain Trail.

How well his idea worked is difficult to determine because he gave it up when a female spiritualist informed him that she had divined the presence of gold in Paradise Park on Rocky Mountain National Park's southern boundary. Together they went off to strike it rich, but no sign of them or gold can be found in Paradise Park today. The ruins of Sam's log cabin and barn, however, still remain in Big Meadows.

Hiking northeast on the Green Mountain Trail, you will find that the approach to Sam's old ranch is relatively wide, free of rocks, and gentle of grade. The trail follows a well-watered gully that is full of a greater than usual variety of plants. In winter, good snow accumulation and a comparatively easy grade make this an excellent trail for ski touring and snowshoeing.

At Big Meadows, head left (north) along the Tonahutu Creek Trail to investigate the remains of Sam's log buildings. Mount Ida is obvious to the north, its left slope seemingly gentle, its right a steep drop-off. Beaver ponds and marsh dominate the foreground. The trail avoids the wet areas, skirting Big Meadows just inside the forest edge.

Continue north to where a path branches steeply left from the Tonahutu Creek Trail, almost a mile from the Green Mountain Trail. Ascend the left branch over a ridge to the Onahu Creek drainage. A clear trail crosses Onahu Creek on a bridge and follows the creek southwest through spruce and fir, lodgepole pine, aspen, and willows down to Trail Ridge Road. A 0.7-mile trail through the woods parallels the road back to your car at Green Mountain Trailhead.

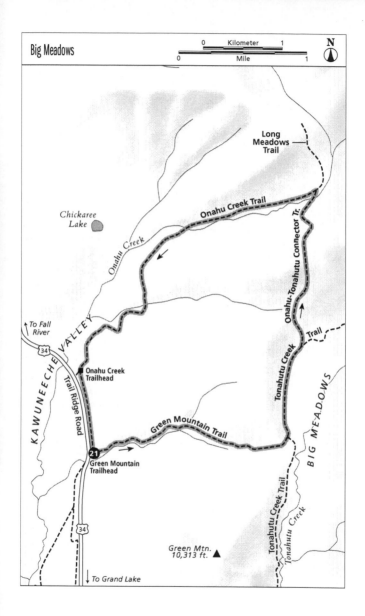

Big Meadows

Chickaree Lake

Onahu Creek

KAWUNEECHE VALLEY

To Fall River

34

Onahu Creek Trailhead

Trail Ridge Road

Onahu Creek Trail

Long Meadows Trail

Onahu-Tonahutu Connector Tr.

Tonahutu Creek

Trail

BIG MEADOWS

Green Mountain Trail

21
Green Mountain Trailhead

Tonahutu Creek Trail

34

Green Mtn. 10,313 ft.

Tonahutu Creek

To Grand Lake

Kilometer
Mile

N

Miles and Directions

0.0 Start at Green Mountain Trailhead.

1.8 Arrive at Big Meadows; turn left onto Tonahutu Trail. (A right turn leads eventually to the park's west-side headquarters and visitor center.)

2.7 Turn left at a fork and ascend Onahu-Tonahutu Connector Trail over the ridge, then descend to Onahu Creek, crossed by a bridge.

6.3 Reach Trail Ridge Road and Onahu Creek Trailhead. find the connecting trail on the left side of the parking lot and continue south to Green Mountain Trailhead.

7.0 Arrive back at Green Mountain Trailhead.

22 Coyote Valley

Short and flat, this walkway amid meanders of the Colorado River can take wheelchair-bound visitors through a variety of water-dependent habitats.

Start: Coyote Valley Trailhead
Hiking time: 2 hours
Distance: 1.6 miles out-and-back
Difficulty: Easy
Trail surface: Packed dirt
Best season: Summer
Other trail users: Wheelchairs
Canine compatibility: Dogs are prohibited
Fees and permits: No fees besides park entrance fee
Trail contacts: Rocky Mountain National Park Backcountry Office,

1000 US Hwy 36, Estes Park; (970) 586-1242; www.nps.gov/romo
Maps: Trails Illustrated Rocky Mountain National Park; USGS Grand Lake
Highlights: Colorado River, views of Never Summer Range, wildlife
Wildlife: Elk, mule deer, moose, coyote, black-billed magpie
Coyote Valley Trailhead elevation: 8,846 feet

Finding the trailhead: Coyote Valley Trailhead is on the west side of Trail Ridge Road, 6.1 miles north of the Grand Lake entrance to Rocky Mountain National Park and 14.2 miles southwest of Fall River Pass. GPS: N40 20.67' / W105 51.50'

The Hike

Of the 297 bridges that carry hikers over streams in Rocky Mountain National Park, the bridge at the beginning of the Coyote Valley Trail may be the most elaborate, a humbler version of the magnificent Carriage Path bridges in Acadia National Park. This structure across the Colorado River leads to a wheelchair-accessible path along the level

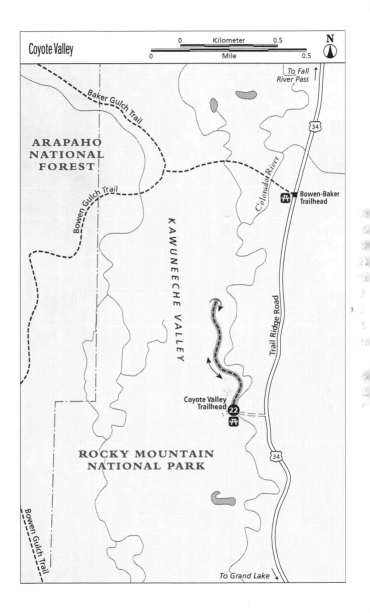

Coyote Valley

Kilometer

0   0.5

Mile

0   0.5

*To Fall
River Pass*

34

Colorado River

Bowen-Baker
Trailhead

**ARAPAHO
NATIONAL
FOREST**

Baker Gulch Trail

Bowen Gulch Trail

K A W U N E E C H E   V A L L E Y

Trail Ridge Road

Coyote Valley
Trailhead

22

**ROCKY MOUNTAIN
NATIONAL PARK**

34

Bowen Gulch Trail

To Grand Lake

floodplain. Many benches and signs help visitors to appreciate and understand the riverside environment on the west side of Rocky Mountain National Park. Broad loops, detours, and cul-de-sacs provide variety in hiking to the trail's end and back.

Miles and Directions

0.0 Start at Coyote Valley Trailhead.

0.8 Arrive at trail's end. Turn around to retrace the route.

1.6 Arrive back at Coyote Valley Trailhead.

23 Cascade Falls

The trail to Cascade Falls is mostly unchallenging for children, but keep them off dangerously alluring slick rocks (all riverside rocks) at the falls.

Start: North Inlet Trailhead
Hiking time: About 4 hours
Distance: 7.0 miles out-and-back
Difficulty: Easy
Trail surface: Dirt
Best season: Summer
Other trail users: Equestrians
Canine compatibility: Dogs are prohibited
Fees and permits: No fees besides park entrance fee
Trail contact: Rocky Mountain National Park Backcountry Office, 1000 US Hwy 36, Estes Park;

(970) 586-1242, www.nps.gov/romo
Map: Trails Illustrated Rocky Mountain National Park; USGS Grand Lake
Highlights: Cascade Falls, North Inlet Creek
Wildlife: Moose, elk, mule deer, yellow-bellied marmot, foxes, mountain chickadee
North Inlet Trailhead elevation: 8,545 feet
Cascade Falls elevation: 8,840 feet

Finding the trailhead: Drive east for 0.3 mile from US 34 toward the town of Grand Lake on CO 278 (Tunnel Road) to where the road forks. Take the left-hand fork, which bypasses the town and leads eventually to East Inlet Trailhead. Leave CO 278 at 0.8 mile from the fork, turning left onto a narrow, unpaved road. A short distance along the unpaved road is a parking area on the left for the Tonahutu Creek Trail. Continue beyond that parking area, go over a hill, turn right, and cross a bridge over Tonahutu Creek. The parking area for North Inlet Trailhead is just beyond the bridge. Often the lot is full, necessitating a turnaround for whatever available parking is nearest, which may even be down at CO 278. GPS: N40 15.30' / W105 48.88'

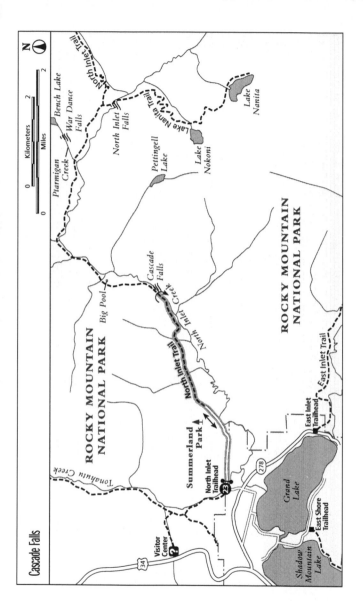

Cascade Falls

The Hike

From the trailhead, walk east on a road along a mostly level grade to Summerland Park, passing through private property. Yellow-bellied marmots are common at Summerland Park. Many hikers also encounter mule deer and moose, thrown in for the thrill. The road narrows to an easy trail beyond Summerland Park, passing through the remains of a lodgepole pine forest where mountain pine beetles have killed many trees, removing shade and making the route warm. On windy days, dead trees may fall across the trail: beware. The North Inlet Trail soon encounters and follows North Inlet Creek, so named because it enters Grand Lake on its northeast shore beyond CO 278.

Hikers usually hear the falls before they come upon a fork in the trail; the two branches unite above Cascade Falls. To avoid conflicts with equestrians, take the right-hand (lower) fork to the falls and return via the upper fork. There will likely be a sign in place a few yards to the right of the lower fork to indicate the way to the falls.

Photographers may seek the best falls viewpoint by climbing—with extreme care—downstream over boulders that frequently are wet and slick. Falling in at this point could cause a photographer to drown, as well as do considerable damage to a camera. Of course, keep kids off the streamside rocks.

Local opinion maintains that the North Inlet Trail to Cascade Falls is mountain lion country. This dubious reputation came about due to a 1997 tragedy when a lion killed a 10-year-old boy, who was out of sight of his parents for perhaps a minute, on this normally safe trail. Hounds trained for lion tracking treed the cat, and rangers killed it.

A roaming lion's range is huge and mule deer are its favored prey. Mule deer are nearly everywhere in the national park except the at highest altitudes. Lion sightings, however, are very rare. Hikers often see deer along the North Inlet Trail in edge areas where meadow meets forest. Another lion sighting here would be headline worthy, but not on the front page above the fold.

"Cascade Falls" seems like a redundant name, but there are countless waterfalls with the same name across the country wherever there are variations in elevation.

Miles and Directions

0.0 Start at North Inlet Trailhead.

0.85 Meet North Inlet Creek.

1.2 Enter Summerland Park (buildings).

3.5 Arrive at the trail fork below Cascade Falls. Head right to explore the falls. Return along the Upper Fork of the North Inlet Trail.

7.0 Arrive back at North Inlet Trailhead.

24 Adams Falls

A gentle trail leads to a misty falls within a spectacular defile.

Start: East Inlet Trailhead
Hiking time: 90 minutes
Distance: 0.6-mile out-and-back
Difficulty: Easy
Trail surface: Dirt
Best season: Summer
Other trail users: Equestrians
Canine compatibility: Dogs are prohibited
Fees and permits: None
Trail contacts: Rocky Mountain National Park Backcountry Office, 1000 US Hwy 36, Estes Park;

(970) 586-1242; www.nps.gov/romo
Maps: Trails Illustrated Rocky Mountain National Park; USGS Shadow Mountain
Highlights: Adams Falls
Wildlife: Gray jay, water ouzel, mountain chickadee
East Inlet Trailhead elevation: 8,391 feet
Adams Falls elevation: 8,470 feet

Finding the trailhead: East Inlet Trailhead is at the end of Tunnel Road (CO 278). Take CO 278 east from US 34 at the village of Grand Lake. After 0.3 mile, take the left fork to bypass the town and head directly to Adams Tunnel, a link in the Colorado–Big Thompson Irrigation Project. Follow more than 2 miles of paved road to the West Portal of Adams Tunnel. (The west end of the tunnel is at the East Inlet to Grand Lake, a minor point of confusion.) At the West Portal bear left on the unpaved road to the trailhead parking area. GPS: N40 14.39' / W105.48.02'

The Hike

The easy walk to Adams Falls rises gradually amid lodgepole pines and glacially deposited boulders. Adams Falls is within

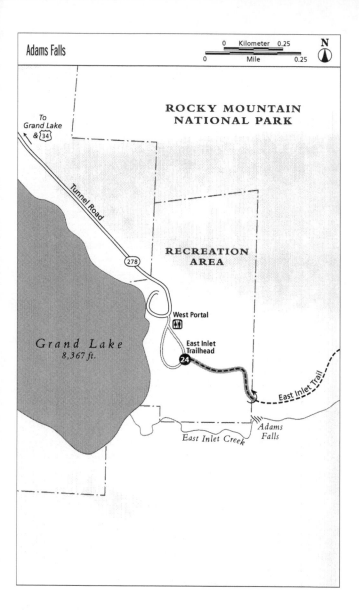

a gorge that evidently follows a geologic crack formed during the uplift of the Rockies and subsequently altered by glacial scouring and water erosion. Splashing through this defile, East Inlet throws up much spray, which can form rainbows around the falls. To see a rainbow, you must have the sun behind you as you look at the water droplets in the air.

Rocks around Adams Falls are smooth, steep, and often wet, all of which contribute to treacherous footing. Parents should take care that their children do not slip into the stream and get washed over the brink. Although the falls make a lovely photo subject, I have made more photos at Adams Falls picturing the rescue of a woman who slipped on the slick rocks and broke her arm falling to the ground, never touching the water. She remained conscious and in courageous spirits throughout the rescue on a wheeled litter. Despite the relative closeness of the road and comparative gentleness of the terrain, her extraction from the wilderness edge seemed long and complicated, inspiring me to be cautious when I hike deep into the wilderness.

Miles and Directions

0.0 Start at East Inlet Trailhead.

0.3 Arrive at Adams Falls.

0.6 Arrive back at East Inlet Trailhead.

Winter Trails

Winter in the park is not exactly quiet. When the wind does not drown the chatter of chickadees, nuthatches, and squirrels, the rhythmic swish of cross-country skis or the creak-crunch of snowshoes lulls backcountry travelers. Although few of its wildlife inhabitants truly hibernate, the park itself seems peacefully drowsy, if not actually asleep.

Winter visitors can appreciate the beauty and fun available for snatching on short days. Visitors should also appreciate the potential hazards of winter, which are more intimidating than in the gentle Rocky Mountain wilderness of summer. In winter, you do not have to worry about lightning, but snow, wind, cold, and ice add the need for even greater caution than in summer.

I would not mention that ice is slick, except that I have experienced some really dumb and potentially fatal falls by dreamily overlooking this seemingly obvious reality. Ice carved the beauty of Rocky Mountain National Park, and enough ice remains to make winter footing hazardous for the incautious. Frozen waterfalls are particularly dangerous, but stream courses that make good winter routes also occasionally have slick spots barely covered by snow or swept bare by wind.

Lake ice can be thin near inlets and outlets. Hikers, snowshoers, and skiers should travel far apart to lessen the stress on the ice and to make aid available to the unlucky one (hopefully just one) who ends up in frigid water.

Enos Mills, the father of Rocky Mountain National Park, wrote, "In winter I discovered solitude, boiled down, refined, and twenty-two carat." Despite this praise, traveling alone in the backcountry in winter is a bad idea. Sharing the glories of the winter backcountry with a companion increases the enjoyment of those delights for everyone, and companions can provide help in case of trouble.

This is especially true of getting caught and buried by an avalanche. Chances of survival decrease by 50 percent after burial for a half hour; the help available at the time of the avalanche is likely to be the only help that will matter. The National Park Service recommends that each member of a winter travel group carry a light shovel in avalanche country. Lacking a shovel, companions can dig effectively with skis and snowshoes. Of course, rescuers should dig with all possible speed, but watch out for subsequent slides. Travel far apart when crossing potential avalanche areas to reduce chances that more than one person can be hit.

Most winter travelers injured or killed by avalanches trigger the slides themselves. You can avoid loosening unstable masses of snow by not crossing open slopes that have a pitch of 30 to 45 degrees, where avalanches most frequently occur.

This avoidance is easier than might seem likely in the steep terrain of Rocky Mountain National Park. With some disconcerting exceptions, the most dangerous places are the glacier-carved bowls and cliffs along the Continental Divide where wind deposits huge amounts of snow swept from the tundra. Ridges that extend east and west from the Continental Divide can carry the zone of danger to the vicinity of some popular backcountry travel routes. Most valleys and forests are safe, but even these slide occasionally.

Just as lightning has repeated strike areas in summer, avalanches tend to plague danger zones repeatedly in winter. Broad vertical bands of treeless avalanche runs are easy to spot. Somewhat more subtle are broken small trees and branches. A hollow sound under snowshoes or skis is not reassuring, especially on the east and north sides of ridges where wind tends to drop snow. Snowballs rolling down the slope from your feet is a bad sign. Cracks opening and lengthening is a very bad sign of slab avalanche, calling for immediate, cautious departure from the area.

If you trigger an avalanche, ditch your pack, ski poles, and skis or snowshoes, and try to use a swimming motion to stay atop the snow. If you go under, protect your nose and mouth with your hands to preserve a breathing space.

By definition, park visitors are not around the park all the time and therefore may not be aware of previous weather conditions that increase avalanche hazards. Because there are no obvious signs of this danger, it is a good idea to check with park staff about recent weather history before venturing into potential avalanche areas, especially those not detailed in this book. Recent snowstorms account for 80 percent of avalanches. The gloriously clear and even windless day may be dangerously deceptive to the person who was not present to experience the previous day's howling blizzard. Long periods of cold temperatures can increase the period of instability leading to avalanches.

Returning to statements of deep profundity, temperatures tend to be cold in winter. To your body, cold and wind are pretty much the same thing, and bitter winds are frequent in Rocky Mountain National Park. Winds of 100 miles per hour are not unusual. The difference between pleasant winter briskness on the lowlands and killing windy cold on the heights can be extreme.

Always carry more clothing than you think you will need. Proving that the mind is the first thing to go when the body tires of struggling through snow, jackets sometimes remain in packs while their owners are at least very uncomfortable and perhaps dying from the cold. Remember to add and subtract the layers of clothing you carry. At least two sets of gloves are light, easy insurance against one pair becoming useless after getting wet. Heavy boots are more appropriate in winter than in summer.

Colorado has the nation's highest rate of skin cancer due to the state's high altitude and resulting thin air and low protection from solar radiation. The danger of solar radiation causing painful sunburn, aging skin, and possibly fatal cancer is even greater in the cold of winter than the warmth of summer. The angle of sunlight is lower in winter, which cuts down on exposure to radiation, but the weather tends to be clearer all day in winter than in summer, reducing the shielding effect of clouds. Snow reflects most of the solar radiation that hits it, almost doubling the dose your skin receives and directing that radiation to parts of your face that normally are shaded from direct sun and thus unprotected by the skin's natural defenses.

Every day, eliminate this danger by applying sunscreen with a high sun protection factor. This is the simplest, easiest, and most beneficial safety action you can take while enjoying the beautiful solitude of winter trails in Rocky Mountain National Park.

25 Winter Hike to Cub Lake

Likely little snow will cover the trail on its flat lower section. As you climb through burned forest, ice or deep snow may make snowshoes handy.

Start: Cub Lake Trailhead
Hiking time: 3 hours
Distance: 4.6 miles out-and-back
Difficulty: Moderately easy
Trail surface: Dirt likely bare at beginning; snow as you begin to climb
Best season: Winter
Other trail users: Human foot traffic only
Canine compatibility: Dogs are prohibited
Fees and permits: No other fees besides park entrance fee

Trail contacts: Rocky Mountain National Park Backcountry Office, 1000 US Hwy 36, Estes Park; (970) 586-1242; www.nps.gov/romo
Maps: Trails Illustrated Rocky Mountain National Park; USGS McHenrys Peak and Longs Peak
Highlights: Ice patterns, wildlife, Cub Lake
Wildlife: Mule deer, elk, coyote
Cub Lake Trailhead elevation: 8,080 feet
Cub Lake elevation: 8,630 feet

Finding the trailhead: From the Beaver Meadows entrance (US 36) to Rocky Mountain National Park, drive 0.2 mile to Bear Lake Road. Follow it for 1.2 miles and turn right toward Moraine Park Campground. Follow the signs for 2.2 miles to the Cub Lake Trailhead. GPS: N40 21.40' / W105 36.90'

The Hike

Famous in summer for flowers, butterflies, and birds, the Cub Lake Trail presents a different but still fascinating face in winter. The lushness of summer falls away, leaving a scene dominated by angular patterns, bold shapes, and subdued tones rather than the individual splashes of brightly colored flora and fauna that attract attention in warm months.

For more than a mile, the trail is mostly flat and easy, usually with little snow. The last mile is steeper. Ice or sections of deep snow can make the way difficult, requiring snowshoes or skis.

Naked water birch and low water make the banks of the Big Thompson River near the trailhead more sharply defined. Because few large boulders break up the flow of this part of the river, the river itself actually is more interesting in winter when water undercuts patterns of ice ledges.

Where the trail leaves thickets and meadows behind as it enters ponderosa pine and Douglas-fir woods, watch for large boulders perched on broad slabs of rock. These are glacial erratics, dropped when the most recent ice sheet melted some 10,000 years ago. In the background is the South Lateral Moraine, the long, dark ridge for which Moraine Park is named.

If snow does not lighten the trees on the north slope, the moraine in winter can be a dark, simple background for photos of the massive granite erratics. Shoot south to emphasize their bold shapes with backlighting to create a halolike rim of light around them, contrasting with the dark background.

Although spotting elk, deer, or coyotes is extremely likely anywhere along the first part of the trail, where the path bends west may be the most productive place to watch, especially in late afternoon. Crouching behind a good-sized erratic will make you somewhat less conspicuous and a good deal more patient if you use the rock as protection from the wind.

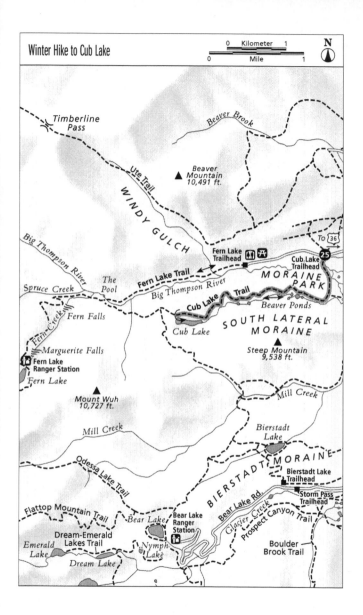

Winter Hike to Cub Lake

Timberline Pass

Beaver Brook

Beaver Mountain 10,491 ft.

Ute Trail

WINDY GULCH

Big Thompson River

The Pool

Spruce Creek

Fern Lake Trailhead

Cub Lake Trailhead

MORAINE PARK

To 36

Fern Lake Trail

Big Thompson River

Cub Lake Trail

Beaver Ponds

SOUTH LATERAL MORAINE

Fern Falls

Fern Creek

Cub Lake

Steep Mountain 9,538 ft.

Marguerite Falls

Fern Lake Ranger Station

Fern Lake

Mount Wuh 10,727 ft.

Mill Creek

Mill Creek

Bierstadt Lake

Odessa Lake Trail

BIERSTADT MORAINE

Bierstadt Lake Trailhead

Storm Pass Trailhead

Flattop Mountain Trail

Bear Lake

Bear Lake Ranger Station

Bear Lake Rd.

Glacier Creek

Prospect Canyon Trail

Dream-Emerald Lakes Trail

Emerald Lake

Nymph Lake

Boulder Brook Trail

Dream Lake

Kilometer 1

Mile 1

N

At the lake, the best scenic shot is from the east shore, looking toward Stones Peak. Find some interesting fallen tree or rocks as foreground. Burned trees contrasting with snow might be interesting on a cloudy day.

Miles and Directions

0.0 Start at Cub Lake Trailhead.

0.5 Turn right on Cub Lake Trail where a trail used mainly by horses in summer turns left.

2.2 Arrive at the east end of Cub Lake.

2.3 Reach the west end of Cub Lake.

4.6 Arrive back at Cub Lake Trailhead.

26 The Pool in Winter

The trail to The Pool follows the Big Thompson River, stilled from its summer chatter by the cold of winter, as foreground trees and shrubs stand out against the shadowed north-facing slope across the river.

Start: Road closure beyond Cub Lake Trailhead
Hiking time: 3 hours
Distance: 5.0 miles out-and-back
Difficulty: Easy
Trail surface: Dirt likely most of the way, snow in a few shaded areas
Best season: Winter
Other trail users: Human foot traffic only
Canine compatibility: Dogs are prohibited
Fees and permits: No fees besides park entrance fee

Trail contacts: Rocky Mountain National Park Backcountry Office, 1000 US Hwy 36, Estes Park; (970) 586-1242; www.nps.gov/romo
Maps: Trails Illustrated Rocky Mountain National Park; USGS McHenrys Peak
Highlights: Arch Rocks, The Pool
Wildlife: Mule deer, elk, red squirrel, mountain chickadee
Trailhead elevation: 8,155 feet
The Pool elevation: 8,320 feet

Finding the trailhead: From Beaver Meadows entrance (US 36) to Rocky Mountain National Park, drive 0.2 mile on Bear Lake Road. Turn left and follow Bear Lake Road for 1.2 miles; turn right toward Moraine Park Campground. Follow the signs for 2.3 miles to a road closure just beyond Cub Lake Trailhead. GPS: N40 21.43' / W105 37.17'

The Hike

The Pool is a water pocket in the Big Thompson River just below its confluence with Spruce and Fern Creeks. The spot is marked by a bridge across the Big Thompson and is an easy hike at nearly all times of the year. Because the trail is on a south-facing slope, the snow cover is relatively slight or absent for most of the winter.

The winter trail begins as 0.8 mile of unpaved, closed road that is open in summer. Most of the closed road passes through stands of quaking aspen. The white aspen trunks are heavily textured with black scars caused by elk stripping off the bark for winter food. You may find elk feeding among these aspen stands.

At Fern Lake Trailhead, the route narrows to a trail surrounded by narrowleaf cottonwood, not a particularly common tree at this elevation. The furrowed cottonwood bark is interesting in the low angle of slanting winter light.

For young children, beaver-cut aspen stumps along the trail make a worthwhile destination about a mile short of The Pool. This playground designed by flat-tailed engineers can fascinate kids for a long time—2 or 3 minutes. Arch Rocks, the very large boulders among which the trail winds along the river, probably were not dropped by retreating glaciers but rather fell from the cliffs above as a result of freezing and thawing water wedging them off.

Beyond Arch Rocks, The Pool is a wide spot where a bridge crosses the Big Thompson River. Of course many pools decorate the length of the Big Thompson River, but this cliff-bound pool is a bit more spectacular than most, even when winter has quieted its whirling torrent.

The Pool gained its particular notoriety through history rather than spectacle. In 1889 a university biological expedition in Moraine Park included Frederick Funston. Although Funston would eventually go on to become a notable general in the Spanish-American War, his virtues of

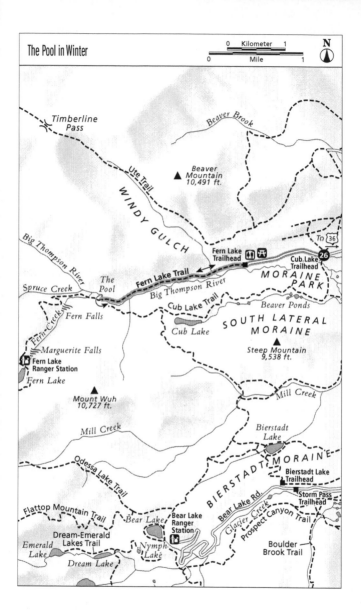

The Pool in Winter

0 Kilometer 1
0 Mile 1

N

Timberline Pass

Beaver Brook

Ute Trail

Beaver Mountain
10,491 ft.

WINDY GULCH

Big Thompson River

Fern Lake Trailhead

To 36

26

Cub Lake Trailhead

MORAINE PARK

Fern Lake Trail

Spruce Creek

The Pool

Big Thompson River

Fern Creek

Cub Lake Trail

Fern Falls

Cub Lake

Beaver Ponds

SOUTH LATERAL MORAINE

Marguerite Falls

Fern Lake Ranger Station

Steep Mountain
9,538 ft.

Fern Lake

Mount Wuh
10,727 ft.

Mill Creek

Mill Creek

Bierstadt Lake

Odessa Lake Trail

BIERSTADT MORAINE

Bierstadt Lake Trailhead

Storm Pass Trailhead

Flattop Mountain Trail

Bear Lake

Bear Lake Ranger Station

Bear Lake Rd.

Glacier Creek

Prospect Canyon Trail

Dream-Emerald Lakes Trail

Nymph Lake

Emerald Lake

Dream Lake

Boulder Brook Trail

command cut no ice with the students on the expedition when he fell into the river. They named the spot Funston Pool, which the US Board of Geological Names shortened to The Pool in 1932.

Miles and Directions

0.0 Start at a road closure beyond Cub Lake Trailhead.

0.8 Arrive at Fern Lake Trailhead.

2.3 Pass between Arch Rocks.

2.5 Arrive at bridge over The Pool.

5.0 Arrive back at the road closure.

27 Skiing to Sprague Lake

This route travels through pleasant woods over moderate terrain, opening to spectacular views with Sprague Lake in the foreground.

Start: Glacier Basin Campground
Hiking time: 3 hours
Distance: 3.0-mile loop
Difficulty: Easy
Trail surface: Snow is often adequate for skiing or snowshoeing
Best season: Winter
Other trail users: Human foot traffic only
Canine compatibility: Dogs are prohibited
Fees and permits: No fees besides park entrance fee

Trail contacts: Rocky Mountain National Park Backcountry Office, 1000 US Hwy 36, Estes Park; (970) 586-1242; www.nps.gov/romo
Maps: Trails Illustrated Rocky Mountain National Park; USGS Longs Peak
Highlights: Sprague Lake
Wildlife: Mule deer, Steller's jay
Glacier Basin Campground Trailhead elevation: 8,590 feet
Sprague Lake elevation: 8,710 feet

Finding the trailhead: From the Beaver Meadows entrance (US 36) to Rocky Mountain National Park, drive about 5 miles along Bear Lake Road to the well-marked entrance to Glacier Basin Campground. Parking is across Bear Lake Road from the campground's entrance. GPS: N40 19.79' / W105 36.75'

The Hike

This may be the most ideal ski trip for beginners on the east side of Rocky Mountain National Park. Three miles round-trip over gentle terrain, the route between Glacier Basin Campground and Sprague Lake usually holds enough snow to cover rocks and logs. During warm spells, though, it could be patchy and icy in some sections, calling for ski removal and a short walk.

This is an excellent short trip for both novice and experienced cross-country skiers or snowshoers. The trail passes through an open meadow and woods, along streams and lakeshore. Although short in distance, the trip may take longer than expected due to frequent stops to enjoy the scenery.

The road into Glacier Basin Campground is blocked at Bear Lake Road in winter. Just beyond the barrier, skiers and snowshoers cross the bridge over Glacier Creek.

Continue up the campground road into a broad meadow with magnificent views of the Front Range. On the opposite side of the meadow are campground C and D Loops. Bear to the left and enter C Loop to campsite 42. From here follow the access path to the Glacier Creek Trail to Storm Pass. Beyond the campsites, brightly colored tags nailed to the trees mark the trail to Sprague Lake. A short way up this trail, the tags become difficult to spot and another trail heads downhill to the right. A sign at this junction indicates the trail to the right goes to Sprague Lake, but do not take this trail. Instead, continue uphill to the left toward Storm Pass. Soon you will spot the bright markers in the trees again. Follow the markers for just over a mile through pleasant woods to a junction where five trails come together. At this somewhat baffling maze, make a sharp right turn (still following the trail markers) for an easy, but exciting ski run to a picnic area at Sprague Lake.

Bear right across the picnic area to a bridge crossing a pond at the west end of Sprague Lake. Follow the trail around the southern shore (to the right). The trip's best photos are from the eastern shore of Sprague Lake. (For

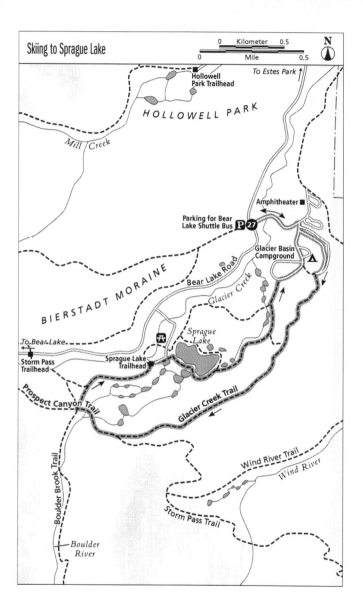

Skiing to Sprague Lake

Hollowell
Park Trailhead

HOLLOWELL PARK

Mill Creek

To Estes Park ↑

Kilometer

Mile

N

Amphitheater ■

Parking for Bear
Lake Shuttle Bus P-27

Glacier Basin
Campground

Bear Lake Road

Glacier Creek

BIERSTADT MORAINE

Sprague
Lake

To Bear Lake

Storm Pass
Trailhead

Sprague Lake
Trailhead

Glacier Creek Trail

Prospect Canyon Trail

Boulder Brook Trail

Wind River Trail

Wind River

Storm Pass Trail

Boulder River

more photo opportunities explore a bit farther along the lake shore beyond where the marked trail departs along a brook back to Glacier Basin Campground.) From the lake's outlet on the east shore, follow trail markers back to D Loop in Glacier Basin Campground.

Miles and Directions

0.0 Begin at entrance to Glacier Basin Campground.

0.5 At Campsite 42 in C Loop, follow access path to Glacier Creek Trail, which leads to Storm Pass.

0.6 Ignore sign indicating trail to right to Sprague Lake and continue uphill toward Storm Pass.

1.7 At maze where five trails come together turn sharply right and follow trail markers in trees for run down to Sprague Lake Picnic Area, then bear right to cross pond at west end of lake. Continue right to follow lake's southern shore.

2.5 At east end of lake, follow trail markers in trees to D Loop in Glacier Basin Campground.

3.0 Arrive back at the entrance to Glacier Basin Campground.

28 Skiing from Glacier Gorge Trailhead to Sprague Lake

Downhill all the way, the trail between Glacier Gorge and Sprague Lake provides a pleasant ski route after recent storms have piled up enough snow.

Start: Glacier Gorge Trailhead
Hiking time: 2 hours
Distance: 3.1-mile shuttle
Difficulty: Moderate
Trail surface: Snow often adequate for skiing or snowshoeing
Best season: Winter
Other trail users: Human foot traffic only
Canine compatibility: Dogs are prohibited
Fees and permits: No fees besides park entrance fee
Trail contacts: Rocky Mountain National Park Backcountry Office, 1000 US Hwy 36, Estes Park; (970) 586-1242; www.nps.gov/romo
Maps: Trails Illustrated Rocky Mountain National Park; USGS McHenrys Peak and Longs Peak
Highlight: Downhill for 3 miles
Wildlife: Red squirrel, mountain chickadee, snowshoe hare
Glacier Gorge Trailhead elevation: 9,230 feet
Sprague Lake elevation: 8,710 feet

Finding the trailhead: Glacier Gorge Trailhead is 8 miles along Bear Lake Road from Rocky Mountain National Park's Beaver Meadows Entrance. The Sprague Lake Picnic Area is about 6.5 miles along Bear Lake Road from US 36 west of the Beaver Meadows entrance to Rocky Mountain National Park. A sign indicates a turn to the left from Bear Lake Road. N40 19.22' / W1105 36.52' (Sprague Lake), N40 18.671' / W105 38.362' (Glacier Gorge Trailhead)

The Hike

Little used by hikers in summer, the trail between Glacier Gorge Trailhead and Sprague Lake is a delightful ski trip when there is enough snow to cover rocks and logs. To take advantage of this one-way downhill route, skiers need to leave cars at Sprague Lake and Glacier Gorge Trailhead. The park's Bear Lake Shuttle does not operate in winter.

The summer trail along the south side of Glacier Creek is not always obvious when covered by snow. Brightly colored markers in trees help to mark the Prospect Canyon Trail to Sprague Lake and beyond to Glacier Basin Campground. The route traverses above the valley floor, encountering various beaver ponds. These supply water to shrubs that will be a severe nuisance to skiers or snowshoers, so strive to keep the ponds to your left.

Do not keep your eyes constantly on your ski tips or snowshoes. Not only will eyes glued to the ground cause you to miss many lovely scenes, but you could also miss your guiding markers in the trees. Failing to look up, around, and ahead may land you in a bothersome natural cul-de-sac of bushes and rocks.

In any case, you are unlikely to stray too far from the trail. For most of the route, the terrain guides you through very pleasant woods. Beyond the beaver pond maze, approximately 3 miles of gentle terrain continue down to Sprague Lake.

Enjoy as abstract sculpture the bold shapes of snow-covered rocks along Glacier Creek and Boulder Brook. The big snows that open this route to skiers and snowshoers can also balance delicate piles of snow on shrub branches. If you get on the trail before the wind picks up, you may encounter some of these snow forms, which make interesting photos.

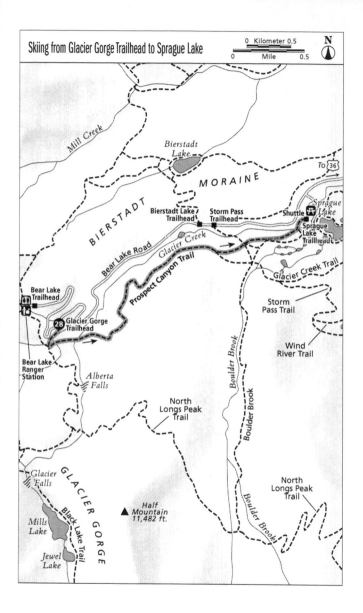

Skiing from Glacier Gorge Trailhead to Sprague Lake

0   Kilometer   0.5

0   Mile   0.5

N

Mill Creek

Bierstadt Lake

MORAINE

To 36

BIERSTADT

Bierstadt Lake Trailhead

Storm Pass Trailhead

Shuttle

Sprague Lake

Sprague Lake Trailhead

Bear Lake Road

Glacier Creek

Prospect Canyon Trail

Glacier Creek Trail

Bear Lake Trailhead

28 Glacier Gorge Trailhead

Storm Pass Trail

Bear Lake Ranger Station

Alberta Falls

Wind River Trail

Boulder Brook

North Longs Peak Trail

Glacier Falls

GLACIER GORGE

Black Lake Trail

Half Mountain 11,482 ft.

Boulder Brook

Boulder Brook

North Longs Peak Trail

Mills Lake

Jewel Lake

Avalanche risk is slight along this route, but skiers and snowshoers do face a couple of stream crossings. Test the ice with a ski pole to make sure that it is strong enough to bear your weight. If in doubt, remove skis or snowshoes and find a way across on rocks and logs.

Miles and Directions

0.0 Start at west end of trailhead parking lot and descend on Glacier Gorge Trail.

0.3 Descend left on Prospect Canyon Trail.

2.3 Arrive at Glacier Creek Trail.

3.1 Descend to Sprague Lake Picnic Area.

29 Loch Vale

Scenic as the euphonious Loch Vale Trail is in summer, it is even more so when low-angle winter light accents the textures of snow and stone on the peaks.

Start: Glacier Gorge Trailhead
Hiking time: 4 hours
Distance: 6.0 miles out-and-back
Difficulty: Moderately easy
Trail surface: Snow sometimes smoothed to ice by wind
Best season: Winter
Other trail users: Human foot traffic only
Canine compatibility: Dogs are prohibited
Fees and permits: No fees besides park entrance fee
Trail contacts: Rocky Mountain National Park Backcountry Office,

1000 US Hwy 36, Estes Park; (970) 586-1242; www.nps.gov/romo
Maps: Trails Illustrated Rocky Mountain National Park; USGS McHenrys Peak
Highlights: Loch Vale, The Loch
Wildlife: Mountain chickadee, snowshoe hare, red squirrel, gray jay
Glacier Gorge Trailhead elevation: 9,240 feet
The Loch elevation: 10,180 feet

Finding the trailhead: From the Park's Beaver Meadows entrance (US 36), follow Bear Lake Road 8 miles to Glacier Gorge Trailhead. GPS: N40 18.671' / W105 38.362'

The Hike

One of the most popular trails in Rocky Mountain National Park in the summer, the path from the Glacier Gorge Trailhead to Alberta Falls is pleasant for winter travelers. But the frozen falls are probably less interesting than in the summer, and portions of the trail beyond often are swept clear of snow by the

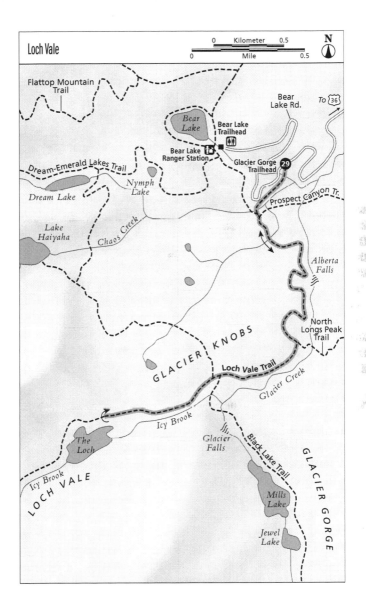

Loch Vale

0   Kilometer   0.5

0   Mile   0.5

N

Flattop Mountain Trail

Bear Lake Rd.

To 36

Bear Lake

Bear Lake Trailhead

Dream-Emerald Lakes Trail

Bear Lake Ranger Station

Glacier Gorge Trailhead   29

Nymph Lake

Prospect Canyon Tr.

Dream Lake

Lake Haiyaha

Chaos Creek

Alberta Falls

North Longs Peak Trail

GLACIER KNOBS

Loch Vale Trail

Glacier Creek

Icy Brook

The Loch

Glacier Falls

Black Lake Trail

Icy Brook

GLACIER GORGE

LOCH VALE

Mills Lake

Jewel Lake

wind. Drifts in other areas may be hip deep. A pattern of on again, off again with snowshoes or skis is likely on this slope.

The wind sometimes howls, raising clouds of snow. You are headed in a southerly direction, so you will be facing into whatever sun there is. Your companions silhouetted against the backlit clouds of blowing snow can make a very dramatic photo. A lens hood will help.

At the Loch Vale–Glacier Gorge trail junction, ignore the steep summer route up Loch Vale. Head left toward Mills Lake as far as Icy Brook, then bear right up the streambed for a snowier route to The Loch. Stay to the right of the stream; ice along the banks sometimes is undercut by dark, frigid water. Plunging through here could dampen your trip. The large spruces and firs in the stream course present lovely forms and textures when clothed in snow. The risk of avalanche along the valley floor is slight, but caution is always necessary, especially after high winds following a snowstorm. This typical pattern may set up unstable snow slopes in atypical locations.

Classic views of Taylor Peak and the Cathedral Wall above The Loch can be more striking in winter, but the lake's island that provides a highlight in summer is less visible in winter. Wind-sculpted limber pines on the lakeshore provide interesting foreground shapes for the view of Taylor Peak.

Miles and Directions

0.0   Start at west end of Glacier Gorge Trailhead parking lot and descend on the Glacier Gorge Trail.

0.9   Arrive at Alberta Falls.

2.2   Trail splits; take middle trail to The Loch in Loch Vale.

3.0   Reach The Loch. Turn around to retrace your steps.

6.0   Arrive back at Glacier Gorge Trailhead.

30 Winter in Glacier Gorge

Traveling mostly south into Glacier Gorge, skiers and snow-shoers squint a lot, but light reflected from the snow fills shadowed areas nearby with attractive light as well as illuminates the ragged peaks surrounding the gorge.

Start: Glacier Gorge Trailhead

Hiking time: 8 hours

Distance: 10 miles out-and-back

Difficulty: Moderate

Trail surface: Snow, sometimes smoothed to ice by wind

Best season: Winter

Other trail users: Human foot traffic only

Canine compatibility: Dogs are prohibited

Fees and permits: No fees besides park entrance fee

Trail contacts: Rocky Mountain National Park Backcountry Office,

1000 US Hwy 36, Estes Park; (970) 586-1242; www.nps.gov/romo

Maps: Trails Illustrated Rocky Mountain National Park; USGS McHenrys Peak

Highlights: Mills Lake, Black Lake

Wildlife: Gray jay, snowshoe hare

Glacier Gorge Trailhead elevation: 9,176 feet

Mills Lake elevation: 9,940 feet

Black Lake elevation: 10,620 feet

Finding the trailhead: Glacier Gorge Trailhead on Bear Lake Road is 8 miles from Rocky Mountain National Park's Beaver Meadows entrance. N40 18.671' / W105 38.362'

The Hike

Trekking to Black Lake is somewhat tiring on a single short winter day. Spring storms may open Black Lake to easier access as days lengthen through April.

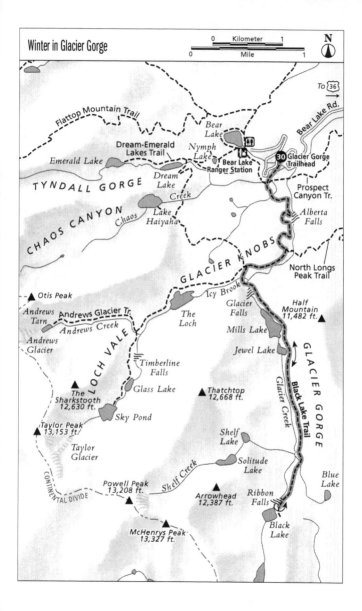

Winter in Glacier Gorge

Kilometer
0   1
0   1
Mile

N

To 36

Flattop Mountain Trail

Bear Lake Rd.

Bear Lake

Dream-Emerald Lakes Trail

Nymph Lake

Bear Lake Ranger Station

30 Glacier Gorge Trailhead

Prospect Canyon Tr.

Emerald Lake

Dream Lake

TYNDALL GORGE

Dream Creek

Alberta Falls

CHAOS CANYON

Lake Haiyaha

Chaos

GLACIER KNOBS

North Longs Peak Trail

Otis Peak

Icy Brook

Glacier Falls

Half Mountain 11,482 ft.

Andrews Tarn

Andrews Glacier Tr.

Andrews Creek

The Loch

Mills Lake

Andrews Glacier

LOCH VALE

Timberline Falls

Jewel Lake

The Sharkstooth 12,630 ft.

Glass Lake

Thatchtop 12,668 ft.

GLACIER GORGE

Taylor Peak 13,153 ft.

Sky Pond

Glacier Creek

Black Lake Trail

Taylor Glacier

Shelf Lake

CONTINENTAL DIVIDE

Powell Peak 13,208 ft.

Shelf Creek

Solitude Lake

Blue Lake

Arrowhead 12,387 ft.

Ribbon Falls

McHenrys Peak 13,327 ft.

Black Lake

The risk of avalanches for winter travelers who ascend along the valley floor of Glacier Gorge is low, but caution always is appropriate.

Where the trail splits to Loch Vale and Glacier Gorge, head left to cross Icy Brook on a bridge and follow the trail into Glacier Gorge.

In winter, when the sun is farther south, the light on Longs Peak above Mills Lake is more dramatic in the afternoon. Unusually shaped trees or rocks against expanses of ice make a frozen lake surface more interesting. However, on the way to Black Lake, it's wise to photograph Longs Peak at Mills Lake in the morning in case storm or wind hide the peaks behind snow on your way back. Hope to reshoot in the afternoon.

Early in the day is the time to photograph McHenry's Peak, which rises directly from Black Lake. Probably the best views of McHenry's will be from farther away, down Glacier Gorge from Black Lake. Put your silhouetted companions, snow-covered rocks, and trees in the foreground. Take lunch on the lip of rock that contains the lake, and look back down Glacier Gorge to note the obvious U-shape of the valley profile, typical of glaciated mountain valleys.

Miles and Directions

0.0   Start at the west end of the Glacier Gorge Trailhead parking lot and descend Glacier Gorge Trail.

0.9   Arrive at Alberta Falls

2.2   Trail splits; take left toward Mills Lake in Glacier Gorge. (The middle trail leads to The Loch; right to Lake Haiyaha.)

2.8   Reach Mills Lake.

5.0   Arrive at Black Lake.

10.0   Arrive back at Glacier Gorge Trailhead.

31 Bear Lake to Hollowell Park

Snow on the route to Hollowell Park often is adequate and shaded by heavy forest after a short ascent on an open, south-facing slope.

Start: Bear Lake
Hiking time: 5 hours
Distance: 4.2-mile shuttle
Difficulty: Moderate
Trail surface: Snow as far as Hollowell Park, then dirt after emerging into open park
Best season: Winter
Other trail users: Human foot traffic only
Canine compatibility: Dogs are prohibited.
Fees and permits: No fees besides park entrance fee

Trail contacts: Rocky Mountain National Park Backcountry Office, 1000 US Hwy 36, Estes Park; (970) 586-1242; www.nps.gov/romo
Maps: Trails Illustrated Rocky Mountain National Park; USGS McHenrys Peak and Longs Peak
Highlights: Bierstadt Lake, delightful woodland trail
Wildlife: Gray jay, snowshoe hare
Bear Lake Trailhead elevation: 9,475 feet
High point: 9,730 feet

Finding the trailhead: Hollowell Park is 3.5 miles from the Beaver Meadows entrance (US 36) to the national park. Bear Lake is 5.5 miles farther at the end of the road. GPS: N40 18.67' / W105 38.67' (Bear Lake); GPS: N40 20.49' / W105 36.31' (Hollowell Park Trailhead)

The Hike

This trail leads to Bierstadt Lake, a popular destination for backcountry travelers in Rocky Mountain National Park in both winter and summer. Frequently during the winter and spring, snowshoes or skis must be carried over some relatively snowless sections when hikers are traveling beyond the lake to meet Bear Lake Road in Hollowell Park.

Bright markers delineate the 4.5-mile route from the Bear Lake parking lot to Hollowell Park. Markers also lead to an alternative destination at the summer parking area for the Bear Lake Shuttle. Begin with a short, steep climb to the trail's high point, about 0.5 mile from Bear Lake. Thereafter the route is downhill for the remaining 4 miles. At the high point the Odessa Lake Trail heads left from the Bierstadt Lake Trail. The National Park Service considers the trail to Odessa Gorge to be avalanche prone.

Continuing on the Bierstadt Lake Trail, be aware that the initial south-facing section through the aspen on the side of boulder-strewn Bierstadt Moraine might not have enough snow to permit snowshoeing or skiing across windswept areas.

Snow conditions generally improve on the broad, gentle top of the moraine. Skiing down a very slight grade amid the lodgepole pine is delightful; the trail in winter often seems more pleasant and interesting than in summer. The repetitive lodgepole trunks form interesting straight line patterns emphasized by the snow.

After a mile of effortless kick-and-glide through the lodgepoles, skiers can detour right to views of Longs Peak across Bierstadt Lake. As in summer, there are no landmarks, and snow may cover the trail signs that guide hikers. However, there probably will be tracks of previous travelers in the snow, and the lake is not hard to find.

Beyond Bierstadt Lake toward Hollowell Park, the trail steepens considerably as it drops through denser north-slope forest along an old logging road. This mile can be challenging for skiers, especially if snow conditions are less than

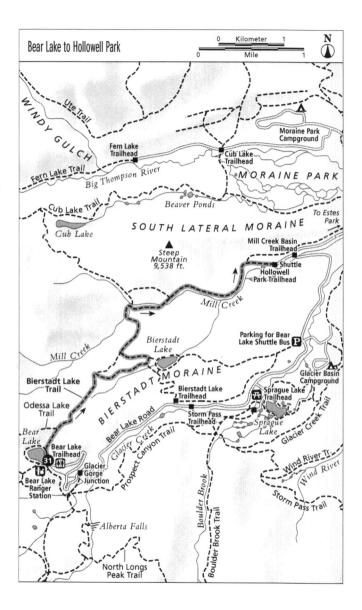

ideal. Be careful; try to maintain a slow, controlled speed to lessen the impact of falls occasioned by protruding rocks or sharp turns.

At Mill Creek, a bridge marks the end of the steepest section of trail. The trail descends past old beaver workings to the broad meadow of Hollowell Park. On the sunnier south-facing slope, the snow frequently does not survive. The last mile out to a car left at the trailhead on the drive up to Bear Lake often involves carrying your skis or snowshoes.

Miles and Directions

0.0 Start at Bear Lake; head right on Bear Lake Nature Trail.

0.1 Ascend right on Flattop Mountain Trail.

0.4 Trail divides; take right branch toward Bierstadt Lake. (Left branch heads up Flattop Mountain.)

1.0 Trail splits; take right branch toward Bierstadt Lake. (Left branch leads down to Mill Creek Basin.

1.4 Trail divides again; view to the right reveals Longs Peak across Bierstadt Lake. Turn left to continue down to Mill Creek Basin.

1.6 Trail steepens as it drops toward Mill Creek Basin and Hollowell Park.

2.6 Trail to left lead to trail west of Moraine Park, particularly to Cub Lake.

4.2 Arrive back at Hollowell Park Trailhead.

32 Skiing to Emerald Lake

Snow hides from winter sun on north-facing slopes, and the frozen surface of Tyndall Creek reposes amid towering peaks and cliffs.

Start: Bear Lake parking area
Hiking time: 4 hours
Distance: 3.6 miles out-and-back
Difficulty: Moderately easy
Trail surface: Snow
Best season: Winter
Other trail users: Human foot traffic only
Canine compatibility: Dogs are prohibited
Fees and permits: No fees besides park entrance fee
Trail contacts: Rocky Mountain National Park Backcountry Office, 1000 US Hwy 36, Estes Park;

(970) 586-1242; www.nps.gov/romo
Maps: Trails Illustrated Rocky Mountain National Park; USGS McHenrys Peak USGS
Highlights: Nymph Lake, Dream Lake, Emerald Lake, wind-shaped limber pines at the lakes
Wildlife: Gray jay, Clark's nutcracker, mountain chickadee, red squirrel
Bear Lake elevation: 9,475 feet
Emerald Lake elevation: 10,080 feet

Finding the trailhead: From the park's Beaver Meadows entrance, follow Bear Lake Road 9 miles to its end at the Bear Lake Trailhead. N40 18.70' / W105 38.70'

The Hike

The most popular hike in the national park during the summer, the lakes above Bear Lake also attract many wilderness visitors in the winter. Using snowshoes or cross-country skis, park visitors find a winter world that is significantly different from summer in the same area.

Visually, the winter woods are cleaner and simpler, with snow covering the natural forest litter such as dead branches and needles. Snow covers intricate details (rocks, leaves, twigs, and bushes), emphasizing the bold, simple shapes of large branches, rocks, and trees.

Avalanches are no threat on the leisurely 0.5 mile to Nymph Lake. Beyond to Dream and Emerald Lakes, the danger is slight, but caution is always a good policy, particularly between Nymph and Dream Lakes. (By contrast, there is more danger from avalanche on the trail between Dream and Haiyaha Lakes, a good reason to take the more popular trail from Dream to Emerald Lakes.)

When snow is adequate on the south-facing summer trail to Nymph Lake, this is the best route. If there are bare patches on this trail, a steeper and less scenic alternative climbs from the west side of Bear Lake through deep woods on a north-facing slope to Nymph Lake.

From the west shore of Nymph Lake, an easy route climbs a narrow valley to Dream Lake, which probably will be adequately frozen to support skiers or snowshoers, though some caution is advisable at the outlet. The firmest ice will be along the lake's south (left) edge. If there are tracks marking firm ice across the lake, follow them. From the west end of Dream Lake, head up the left side of the Tyndall Creek valley for a few hundred yards. Where the grade flattens, cut to the right through trees and continue on to Emerald Lake.

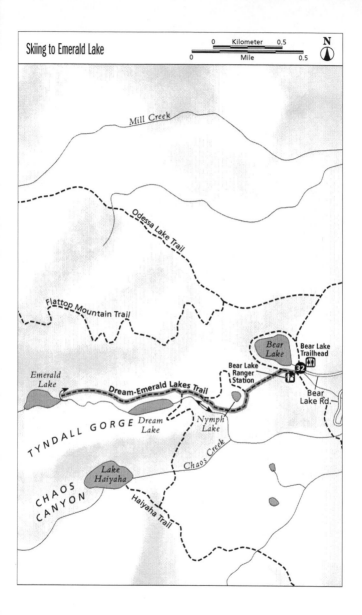

Skiing to Emerald Lake

Mill Creek

Odessa Lake Trail

Flattop Mountain Trail

Bear Lake

Bear Lake Trailhead

Bear Lake Ranger Station

Emerald Lake

Dream-Emerald Lakes Trail

Bear Lake Rd.

TYNDALL GORGE

Dream Lake

Nymph Lake

Chaos Creek

Lake Haiyaha

CHAOS CANYON

Haiyaha Trail

Miles and Directions

0.0 From Bear Lake Parking Lot, head west about 200 yards to lake. Head left around the lake shore to winter trail to Nymph Lake.

0.5 Arrive at Nymph Lake, from west shore ascend a narrow valley to Dream Lake.

1.0 Arrive at Dream Lake to ski across lake to its west end to ascend the left side of Tyndall Creek Valley.

1.3 Head to right through the trees and continue ascending to Emerald Lake.

1.8 Arrive at Emerald Lake.

3.6 Arrive back at the Bear Lake parking lot.

33 Upper Beaver Meadows in Winter

Enough snow for skiing or snowshoeing is uncommon in Upper Beaver Meadows, but not as uncommon as beaver, for which the very common elk and deer provide an appealing substitute.

Start: Barrier at Upper Beaver Meadows Road 0.6 mile from Beaver Meadows entrance to the park

Hiking time: 2 hours

Distance: 3.5-mile loop

Difficulty: Easy

Trail surface: Dirt

Best season: Winter

Other trail users: Equestrians are permitted on the road

Canine compatibility: Leashed dogs are permitted only on road

Fees and permits: No fees besides park entrance fee

Trail contacts: Rocky Mountain National Park Backcountry Office,

1000 US Hwy 36, Estes Park; (970) 586-1242; www.nps.gov/romo

Maps: Trails Illustrated Rocky Mountain National Park; USGS McHenrys Peak

Highlights: Elk exclosure to test effect of grazing, glacial geology

Wildlife: Mule deer, elk, black-billed magpie, raven

Winter Beaver Meadows Trailhead elevation: 8,302 feet

Upper Beaver Meadows Summer Trailhead elevation: 8,440 feet

Finding the trailhead: The closed road into Upper Beaver Meadows begins on US 36 at a major bend 0.6 mile west of the Beaver Meadows entrance to Rocky Mountain National Park. Park in a turnout across US 36 from the trailhead. N40 22.19' / W105 35.52'

The Hike

This easy winter trail offers the option of a 3-mile hike with a canine companion. The out-and-back hike follows the closed road, which winds north of the creek. Hiking with leashed dogs is permitted for 1.5 miles to the road's end at the summer trailhead. Keeping dogs leashed is essential so that park managers will continue to allow hiking with dogs on closed roads.

The meadows are thick with elk and deer, which many unleashed dogs would chase. During the rut, mule deer bucks are likely to gore dogs that annoy them, resulting in very serious injury. Chasing wildlife is the cardinal sin that dogs can commit in a national park, although the deer and elk pay no more attention to leashed dogs than to human hikers. With their vastly superior senses of smell and hearing, leashed dogs may show you wild animals that you would otherwise overlook.

Dogs are not permitted on the trail beyond the end of the road. Hikers with dogs must return along the closed road.

To hike the loop route without dogs, follow a trail that leaves the road to head left just inside the road barricade near US 36. This trail, used mainly by horse riders in the summer, circles clockwise to the summer trailhead at the west end of the road, which leads back to the winter trailhead.

The long, forested ridge defining the south edge of Beaver Meadows is a moraine, a pile of rocks dropped by the melting ice of a glacier between 10,000 and 20,000 years ago. The trailhead sits more or less on the remnants of a moraine dumped by a larger glacier about 100,000 years earlier (a little more obvious directly east across the highway). Obviously, the younger moraine is much bigger. Many

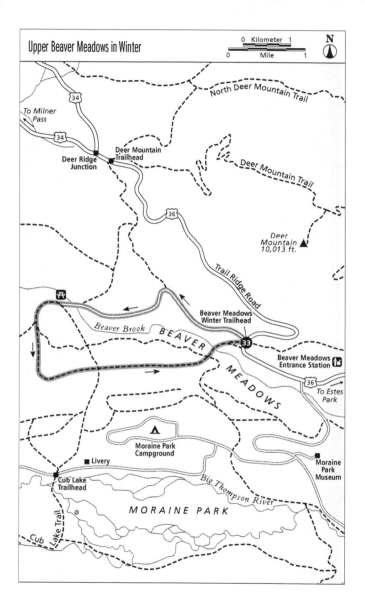

Upper Beaver Meadows in Winter

millennia of erosion of the older moraine account for much of the difference in height.

You are likely to see beavers in many places in the national park but not in Beaver Meadows. Presumably, these large rodents lived here in the late 1800s when homesteaders turned the meadows into irrigated hay fields. In previous centuries, Beaver Meadows was a favored summer campsite for Native Americans, and deadly battles between warring tribes reputedly took place here.

Photographers need a 300mm lens to hunt portraits of deer and elk. Avoid disturbing them by approaching too close. A shorter telephoto lens can be used if the animals are to be an interesting foreground in a photo of distant high peaks early in the morning.

Miles and Directions

0.0 Start at US 36 where a barrier closes the road to Upper Beaver Meadows.

1.5 Road reaches Upper Beaver Meadows Trailhead. Bear left on trail that loops east back to US 36. Bear left toward southern side of loop.

3.5 Arrive back at the barrier at US 36, if hiking without a dog.

34 Winter Travel on Deer Mountain

During much of the winter, the open south-facing slopes of Deer Mountain do not require skis or snowshoes to traverse.

Start: Deer Ridge Junction of US 34 and 36
Hiking time: 5 hours
Distance: 6.0 miles out-and-back
Difficulty: Moderately easy
Trail surface: Snow and dirt constantly switch
Best season: Winter
Other trail users: Human foot traffic only
Canine compatibility: Dogs are prohibited
Fees and permits: No fees besides park entrance fee
Trail contacts: Rocky Mountain National Park Backcountry Office, 1000 US Hwy 36, Estes Park; (970) 586-1242; www.nps.gov/romo
Maps: Trails Illustrated Rocky Mountain National Park; USGS Estes Park
Highlights: Views of Mummy Range and Front Range, picturesque limber pine, Deer Mountain summit
Wildlife: Mule deer, elk, black-billed magpie, mountain chickadee
Deer Ridge Junction elevation: 8,930 feet
Deer Mountain elevation: 10,013 feet

Finding the trailhead: Begin hiking where US 34 and US 36 meet. There is no parking lot, but you can park along the broad shoulders. N40 23.25' / W105 36.66'

The Hike

At some time in almost every Rocky Mountain National Park winter, a long, warm, dry spell makes cross-country skiers and snowshoers despair and think of setting up banana farms near Estes Park. This is the time to hike up Deer Mountain, when you likely will encounter little snow.

During other times, such as when the skiing is good at Bear Lake or Glacier Basin Campground, the north-facing switchbacks on Deer Mountain will still have fairly deep snow. The zigzag nature of the trail causes climbers up Deer Mountain to move constantly from bare trail to snowy trail. On-off, on-off with skis or snowshoes is a significant nuisance.

Once on top, the trail usually holds snow in winter. But during the banana-belt periods, you may be able to walk a more or less dry route all the way. The trail undulates for more than 0.5 mile along the mountaintop to a trail junction where a sharp right turn leads a few steep yards to the summit.

Many of the summer's best views from Deer Mountain are even better in winter. Snow on the high peaks of the Mummy Range to the north and Front Range to the south add considerable drama to these vistas. Low-angle winter light on the peaks gives the mountains more texture than in summer, although the shift of the sun to the south reduces the texture on the Mummy Range.

Ypsilon Mountain, with its classic bowl-shaped cirque cut by glaciers on its face, is the obvious center of interest among the high peaks closest to Deer Mountain. Of course, the Y shaped pattern of snow-filled gullies that gave Ypsilon its name are far less obvious in winter when snow covers the whole face.

Where the trail levels atop Deer Mountain, forest fire has burned twisted limber pines, which are made even more interesting when snow accents the gray, rust, and black patterns. Low winter light is more likely than summer rays to emphasize the rough texture of the raised wood grain.

Mule deer are very common on Deer Mountain. Big bucks look their best in winter. By shredding bark from

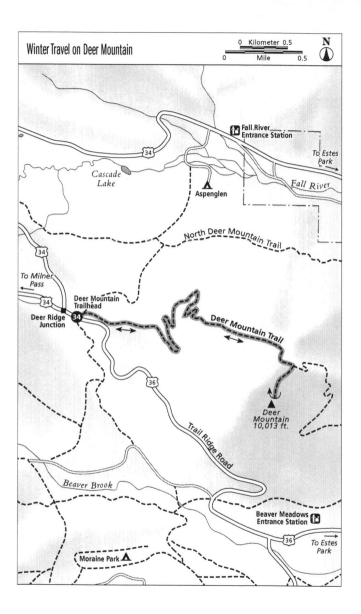

Winter Travel on Deer Mountain

0   Kilometer 0.5

0   Mile   0.5

N

Fall River Entrance Station

To Estes Park

34

Cascade Lake

Aspenglen

Fall River

North Deer Mountain Trail

34

To Milner Pass

34

Deer Mountain Trailhead

34

Deer Ridge Junction

Deer Mountain Trail

Deer Mountain Trail

36

Deer Mountain 10,013 ft.

Trail Ridge Road

Beaver Brook

Beaver Meadows Entrance Station

36

To Estes Park

Moraine Park

inoffensive young trees, the bucks have polished their antlers free of summer velvet. These dueling tools and coyote spikers shine in the winter sun.

Miles and Directions

0.0 Start at the intersection of US 34 and 36 at Deer Ridge Junction.

3.0 Arrive at the summit of Deer Mountain.

6.0 Arrive back at Deer Ridge Junction.

35 Trail Ridge Road

A winter walk up Trail Ridge Road (closed to vehicles above Many Parks Curve) likely exposes hikers to a wide variety of conditions and sights overlooked when driving up the road in summer.

Start: Many Parks Curve
Hiking time: 9 hours
Distance: 12 miles out-and-back
Difficulty: Moderate
Trail surface: Asphalt often covered by snow drifts.
Best season: Winter
Other trail users: Human foot traffic only
Canine compatibility: Leashed dogs are permitted on Trail Ridge Road, after the first Saturday in April, as indicated by signs.
Fees and permits: No fees besides park entrance fee
Trail contacts: Rocky Mountain National Park Backcountry Office,

1000 US Hwy 36, Estes Park; (970) 586-1242; www.nps.gov/romo
Maps: Trails Illustrated Rocky Mountain National Park; USGS Trail Ridge
Highlights: Views of the Mummy Range, wind-sculpted snow, wind- and fire-sculpted trees
Wildlife: White-tailed ptarmigan, mountain chickadee, gray jay
Many Parks Curve elevation: 9,620 feet
Ute Crossing elevation: 11,440 feet

Finding the trailhead: Follow Trail Ridge Road to its closure at Many Parks Curve. NPS does a good job of plowing the two clearly marked nearby parking lots. Drive on to second area to begin hike and to avoid left turn across oncoming traffic lane. GPS: N40 23.28' / W105 37.87'

The Hike

Trail Ridge Road is closed above Many Parks Curve from late October through late May. Fairly easy to walk, the road is the easiest winter route to tree line in Rocky Mountain National Park. Tree line in winter is an interesting area and the place to find white-tailed ptarmigan in their all-white winter plumage.

Avalanche danger is slight; snowshoes or skis are likely unnecessary. Gaiters are handy for occasional wading through drifts, particularly between the open span of the old Hidden Valley ski slope and Rainbow Curve.

Wind can be a howling fury, particularly beyond Rainbow Curve, near tree line. Picking a day with good weather can make the difference between a trip remembered for exciting scenes and wildlife and one remembered for its misery.

The wind often carves snow drifts into interesting abstract patterns in the area of Rainbow Curve. During winter, the sun is low enough in the sky during most of the day to create dramatic shadows that accent the textures of these drifts.

Winter winds have given the trees above Rainbow Curve their fantastic shapes. Forest fire then accented and simplified the shapes by killing many trees. Snow further heightens the drama by covering up extraneous details.

Where the ridgeline narrows at tree line, large rock outcrops create a venturi effect. The same volume of air that has been moving across unobstructed tundra has to push through restricted space in the same amount of time. Therefore, the wind has to blow faster. Speeds well above 100 miles per hour are common and can knock you down. Wind chill can drop temperatures to decidedly dangerous

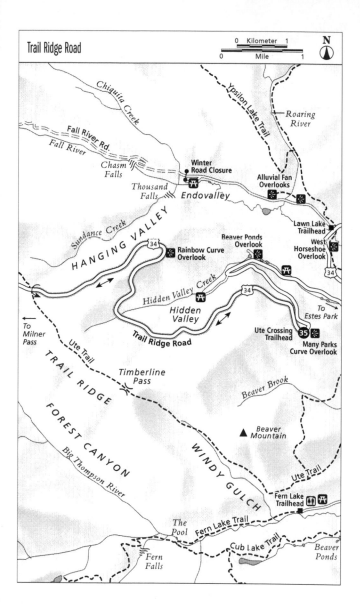

levels, and frostbite is a common hazard. Linking arms with companions to fight your way across the venturi zone can be necessary on some days.

Look for ptarmigan by leaving the road above tree line at Ute Crossing, where a sign explains Native American travel across Trail Ridge. Head uphill across the road from the sign to look for the all-white grouse among scrub willows at tree line. Beware of going too near cliffs above Hanging Valley, particularly if windblown snow blocks your vision and unsteadies your balance.

Miles and Directions

0.0   Start at the Many Parks Curve parking area.

6.0   Arrive at Ute Crossing.

12.0   Arrive back at the Many Parks Curve parking area.

36 Wild Basin in Winter

Lower elevation than trails in the Bear Lake area make skiing or snowshoeing in Wild Basin problematic during much of the winter until backcountry travelers begin ascending from Saint Vrain Creek toward Calypso Cascades and Ouzel Falls.

Start: Winter Wild Basin Trailhead

Hiking time: 6 hours

Distance: 7.4 miles out-and-back

Difficulty: Moderately easy

Trail surface: Snow sometimes adequate for skiing or snowshoeing at beginning, then snow shortly after summer trailhead

Best season: Winter

Other trail users: Human foot traffic only

Canine compatibility: Dogs are prohibited

Fees and permits: No fees besides park entrance fee

Trail contacts: Rocky Mountain National Park Backcountry

Office, 1000 US Hwy 36, Estes Park; (970) 586-1242; www.nps.gov/romo

Maps: Trails Illustrated Rocky Mountain National Park; USGS Allen's Park

Highlights: North Saint Vain Creek, Calypso Cascades, Ouzel Falls

Wildlife: Mountain chickadee, red squirrel, snowshoe hare

Winter Wild Basin Trailhead elevation: 8,350 feet

Calypso Cascades elevation: 9,200 feet

Ouzel Falls elevation: 9,450 feet

Finding the trailhead: Eleven miles south of Estes Park, turn right (west) onto CR 84W, the road to Wild Basin, marked by a sign along CO 7. Drive 0.3 mile to obvious right turn onto unpaved road leading past the national park entrance station. The winter trailhead is a bit more than a mile down this road. GPS: N40 12.80' / W105 33.02'

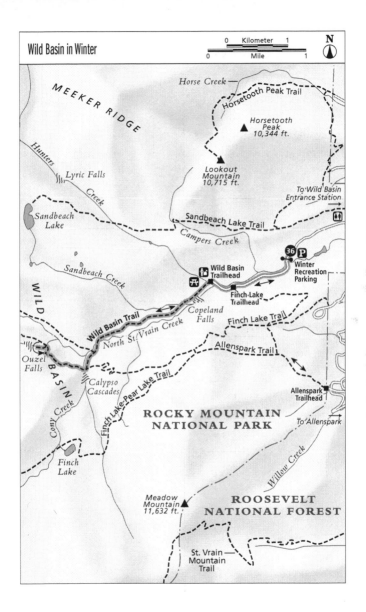

Wild Basin in Winter

Horse Creek

MEEKER RIDGE

Horsetooth Peak Trail

Horsetooth Peak 10,344 ft.

Lookout Mountain 10,715 ft.

To Wild Basin Entrance Station

Hunters Creek

Lyric Falls

Sandbeach Lake

Sandbeach Lake Trail

Campers Creek

Sandbeach Creek

36 P

Winter Recreation Parking

Wild Basin Trailhead

Finch Lake Trailhead

WILD

Wild Basin Trail

Copeland Falls

Finch Lake Trail

North St. Vrain Creek

Allenspark Trail

Ouzel Falls

Calypso Cascades

Allenspark Trailhead

BASIN

Cony Creek

Finch Lake-Pear Lake Trail

ROCKY MOUNTAIN NATIONAL PARK

To Allenspark

Willow Creek

Finch Lake

Meadow Mountain 11,632 ft.

ROOSEVELT NATIONAL FOREST

St. Vrain Mountain Trail

0   Kilometer   1

0   Mile   1

N

The Hike

Even in midwinter, the quality of skiing or snowshoeing in the lower parts of Wild Basin depends on the heaviness of the most recent snowstorm. Relatively low altitude and south-facing exposure make snow on the trail patchy, particularly in spring. But north-facing slopes and heavily forested areas hold enough snow to make skis or snowshoes handy until late spring. Backcountry travelers probably will have to carry their skis or snowshoes over some bare sections.

Avalanche danger is slight in Wild Basin for the first 6 or 7 miles, after which steep slopes create many slide paths.

From the winter parking area, follow the summer road about a mile along North Saint Vrain Creek.

Beyond the summer trailhead the trail follows the creek even more closely than does the road. More than 2 miles from winter parking, a bridge crosses the creek. Here the snow cover increases, and the trail steepens as it climbs to Calypso Cascades. Cross Calypso Cascades (the bridge is usually evident above the snow) and pass through forest burned in 1978.

At Ouzel Creek leave the trail to follow the creek a short way up to Ouzel Falls. Quieted from its summer roar, this waterfall freezes into patterns that rival its summer drama.

Miles and Directions

0.0 Start at winter Wild Basin Trailhead.

2.1 Reach bridge across North Saint Vrain Creek

2.8 Trail turns right to cross Calypso Cascades on a park. (Allenspark Trail enters from left.)

3.7 Reach Ouzel Falls. Turn around to retrace your steps.

7.4 Arrive back at winter Wild Basin Trailhead.

About the Author

Guidebooks by Kent Dannen are the standard reference for the trails of Rocky Mountain National Park. He has hiked every trail in the park and those in this guide many times. Nonetheless, they never get old or fail to offer something new each time he travels these trails. He began his professional guiding activities as hike master and naturalist for the YMCA of the Rockies and has led hundreds of hikes covering thousands of miles. A former contributing editor of *Backpacker Magazine,* he freelances as a writer and photographer. He has taught classes from coast to coast in nature photography, bird identification, and the history of wildlife in America for the National Wildlife Federation and Canadian Wildlife Federation from coast to coast. He also is a recipient of the US Department of Agriculture Certificate of Appreciation for his outstanding volunteer services in developing educational materials that help manage and protect the Indian Peaks Wilderness. Kent Dannen has written six other guidebooks: *Short Hikes in Rocky Mountain National Park, Hiking Rocky Mountain National Park, Best Hikes Rocky Mountain National Park, Best Hikes Colorado's Indian Peaks Wilderness, Hiking Waterfalls Rocky Mountain National Park,* and *Rocky Mountain Wildflowers.* He lives near Allenspark, Colorado.